This

ARABIC WRITING
WORKBOOK

Belongs to:

First Name: .... :الاسم

Last Name: .... :اللقب

Alif Baa Taa

Handwriting Practice Workbook

This is a beginning handwriting book that can be used by adults and kids of all ages.

It is organized in a progressive skill building way to help you (or your children) learn how to draw calligraphic lines and forms of the Arabic language.

Part 1: Begin tracing with lines and curves

Part 2: Learning the Arabic alphabet

       Trace and Practice letters (Alif to yaa)

Bonus Part 3: Tracing the Arabic numbers

Tip:

You can get even more writing practice by creating reusable sheets!

1. Take this book apart.

   Rip off the cover to more easily tear out its pages.

2. Place individual sheets into sheet protectors.

3. Write on the sheets with dry-erase markers.

4. Wipe off the marker to reuse.

Arabic Alphabet

Twenty-Eight Letters

Written from Right to Left

←

ج	ث	ت	ب	أ
Jeem	Thaa	Taa	Baa	Alif

ر	ذ	د	خ	ح
Raa	Thaal	Daal	Khaa	Haa

ض	ص	ش	س	ز
Daad	Saad	Sheen	Seen	Zay

ف	غ	ع	ظ	ط
Faa	Ghayn	Ayn	Dhaa	Taa

ن	م	ل	ك	ق
Nuun	Meem	Laam	Kaaf	Qaaf

ي	و	ه
Yaa	Waaw	Haa

Tracing Lines

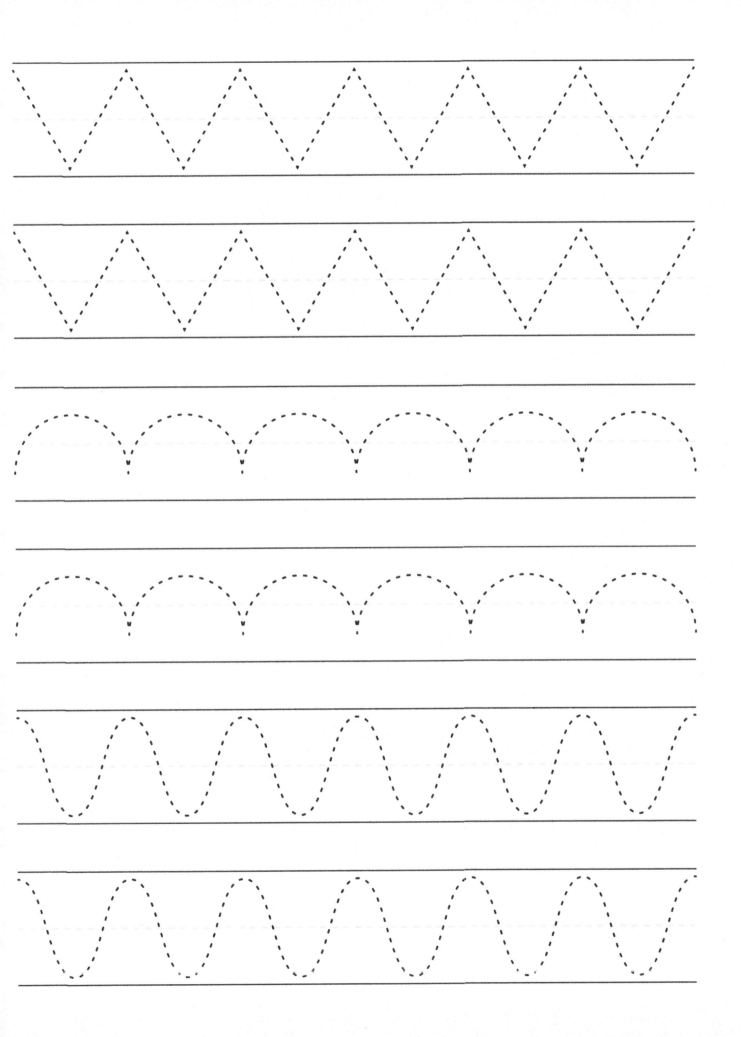

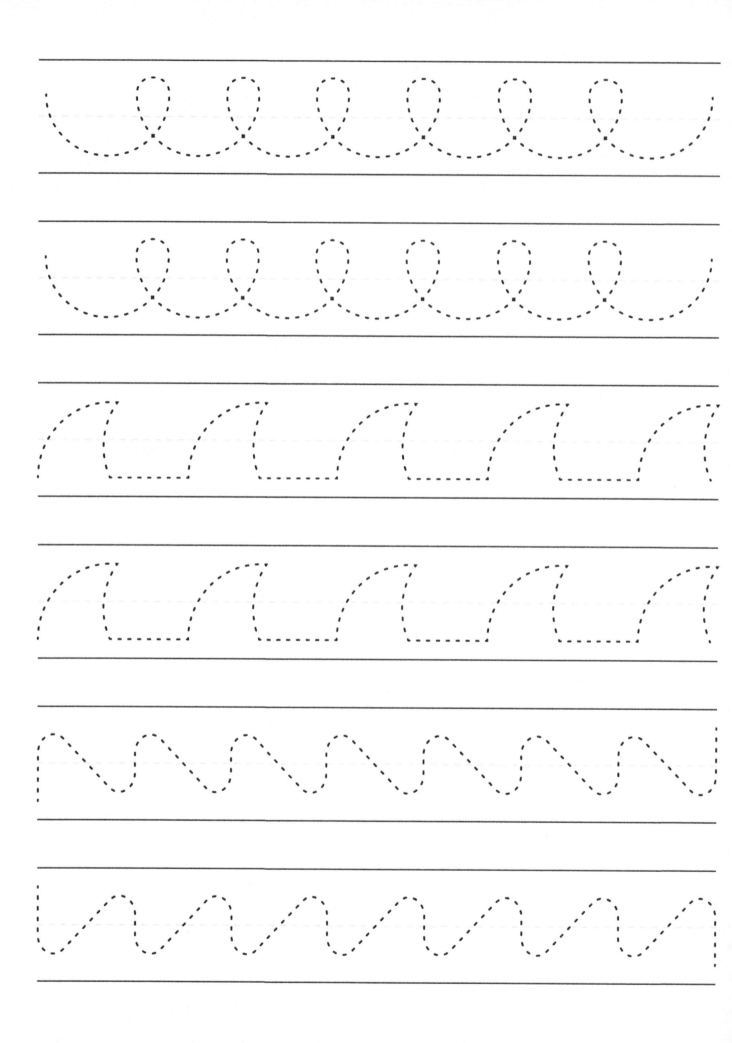

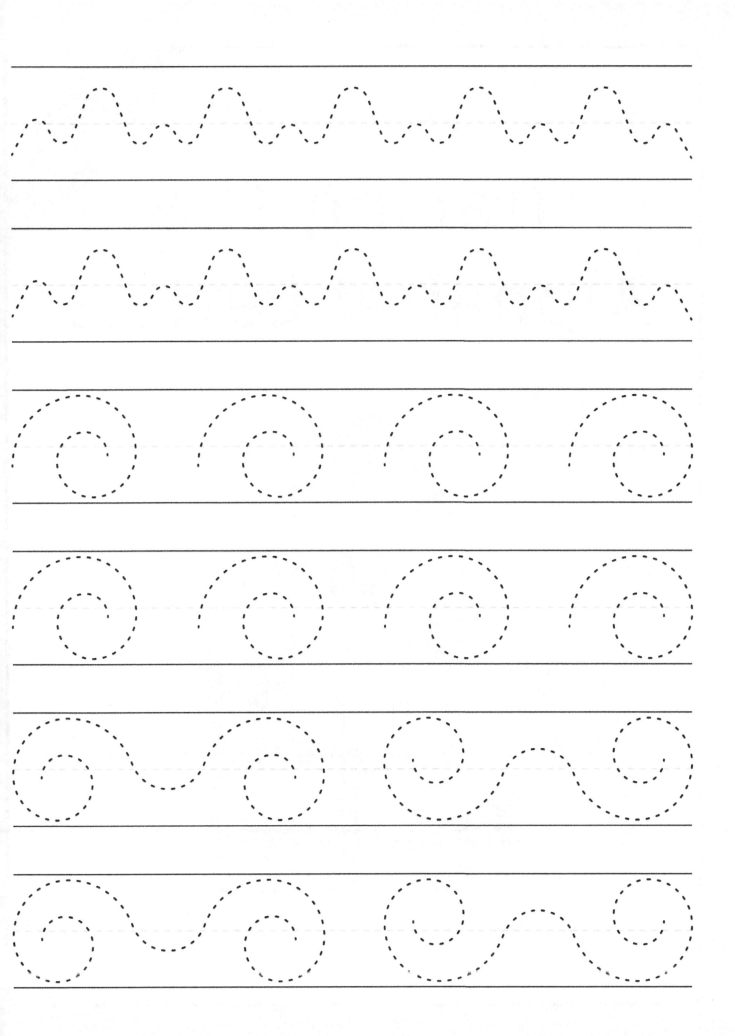

Tracing The Alphabet Letters

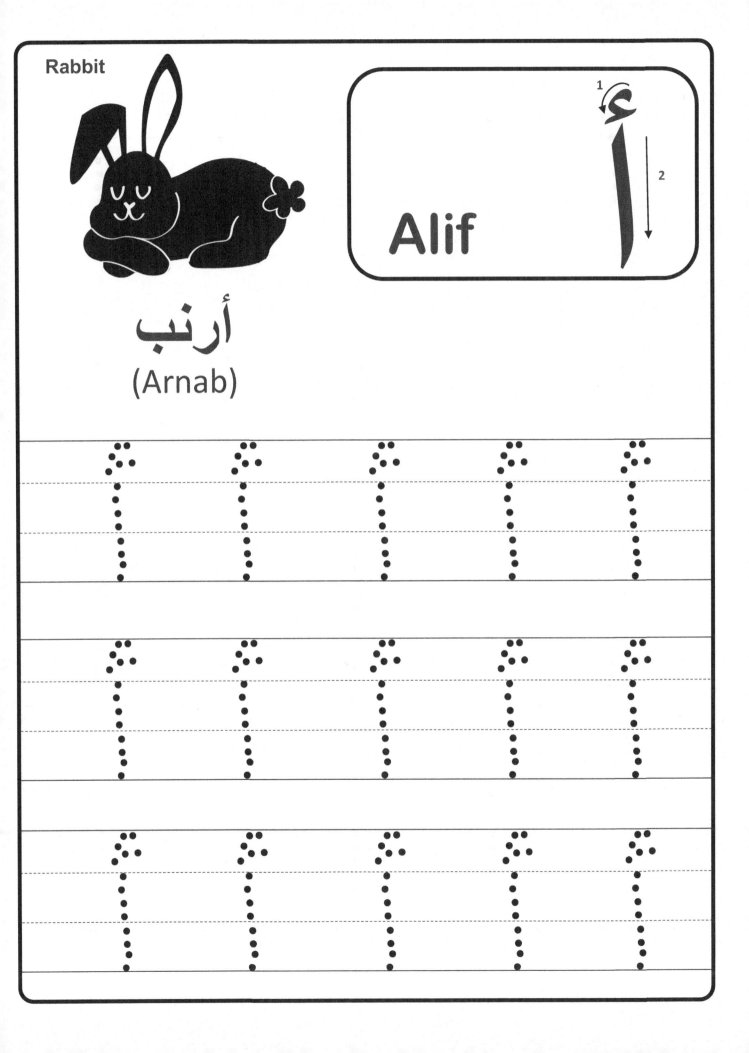

Rabbit

أرنب

(Arnab)

Alif

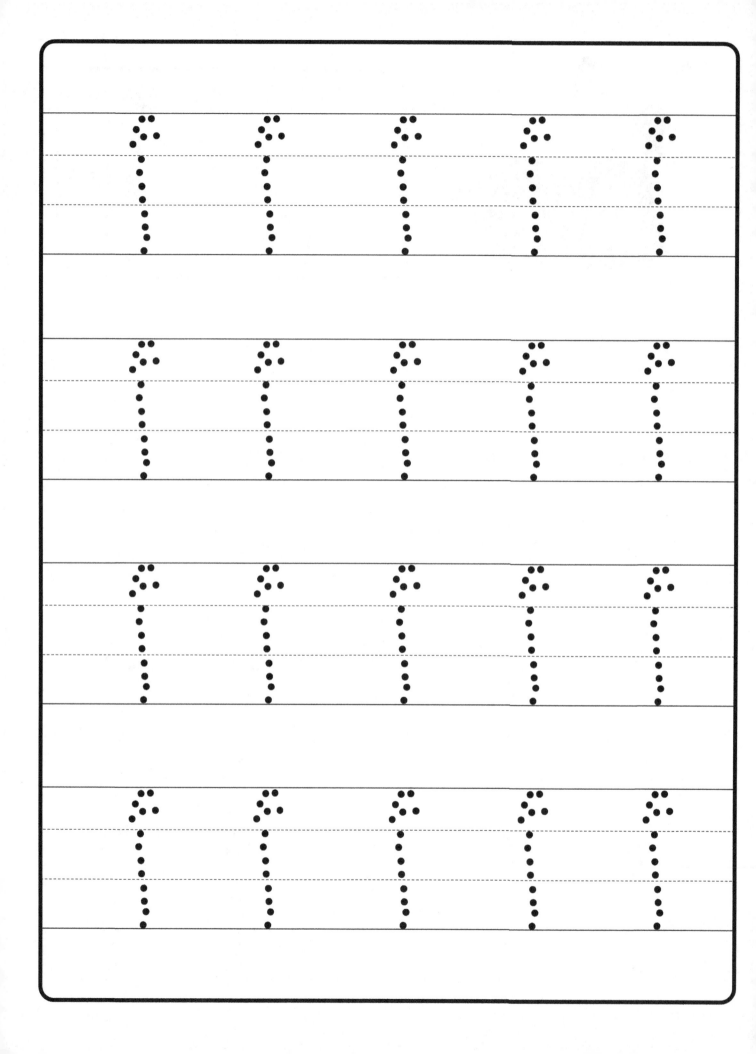

House

Baa

ب

بيت
(Bayt)

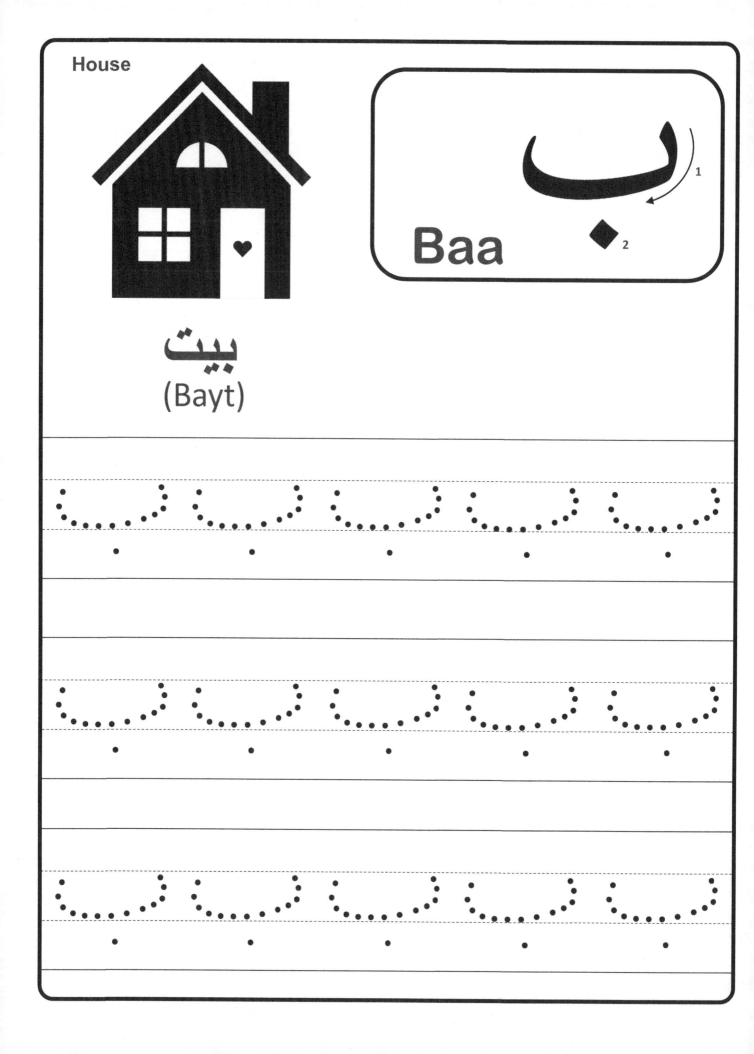

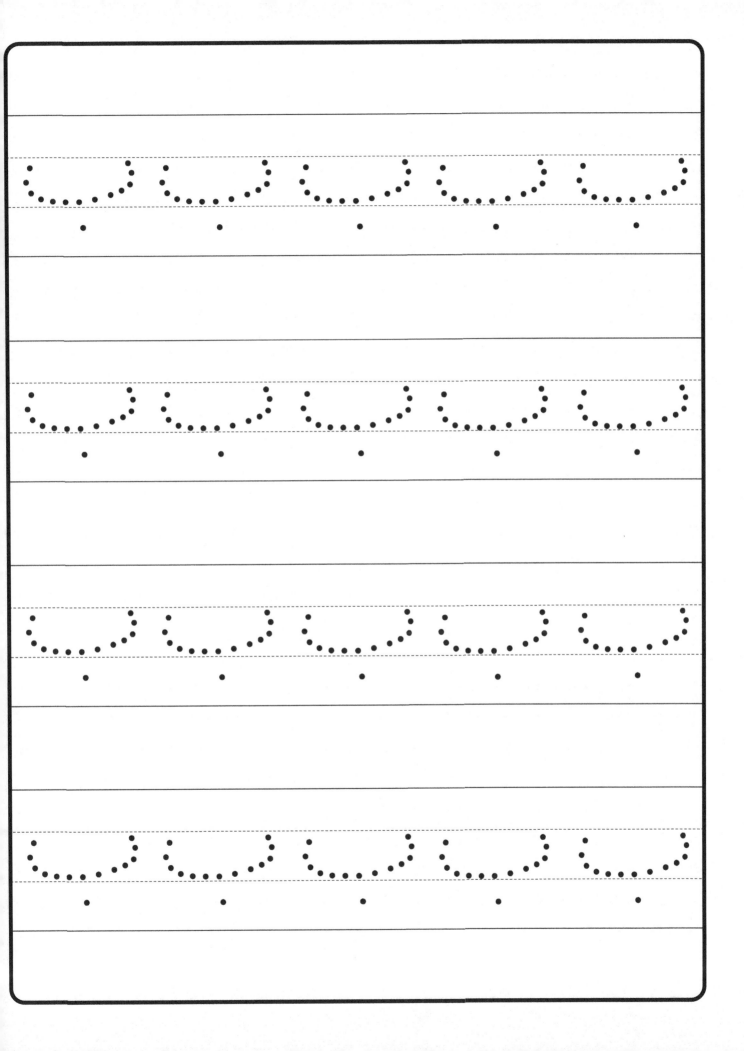

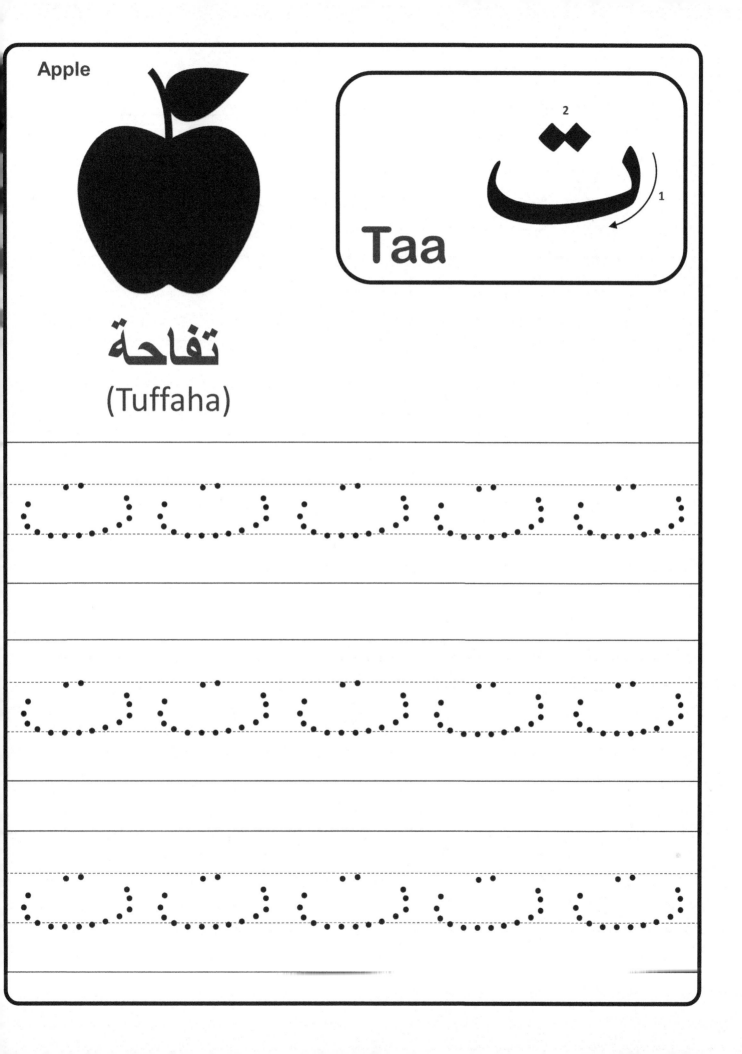

Apple

تفاحة
(Tuffaha)

Taa

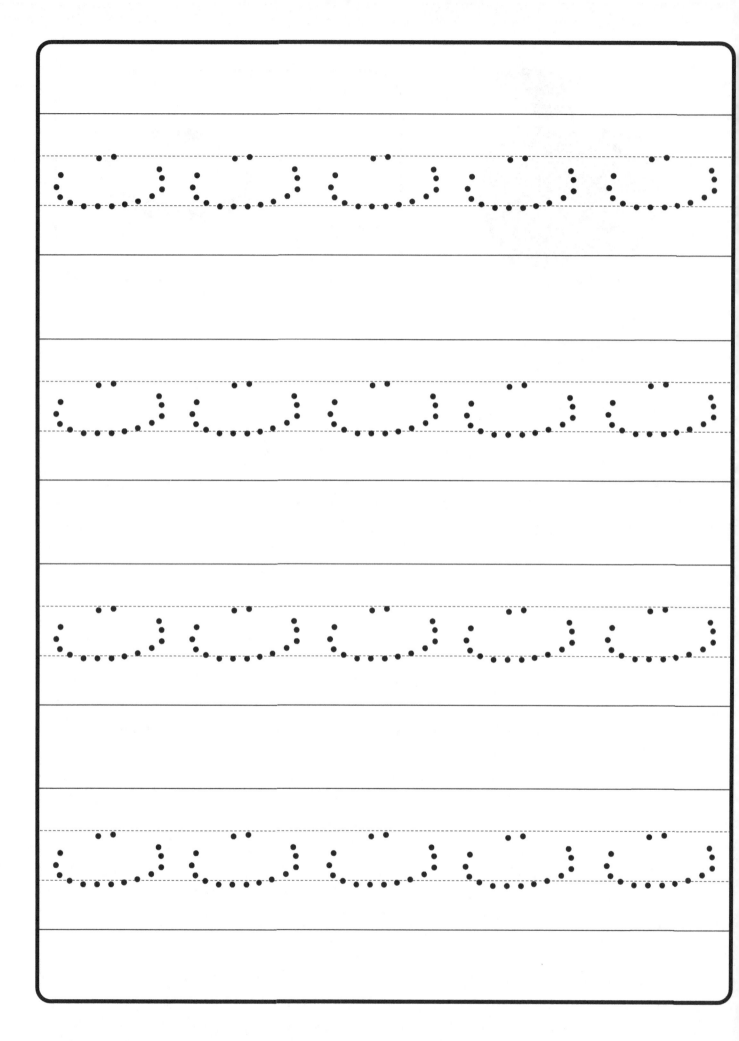

Dress

ث

² ♦
♦
♦

ر 1

Thaa

ثوب
(Thawb)

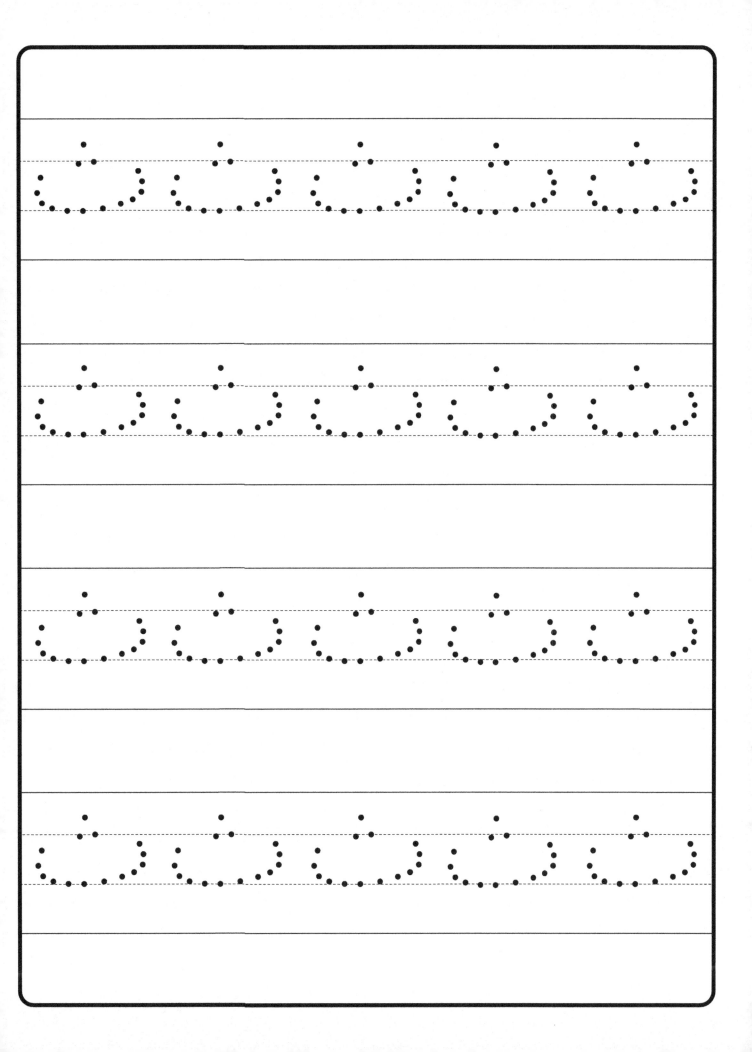

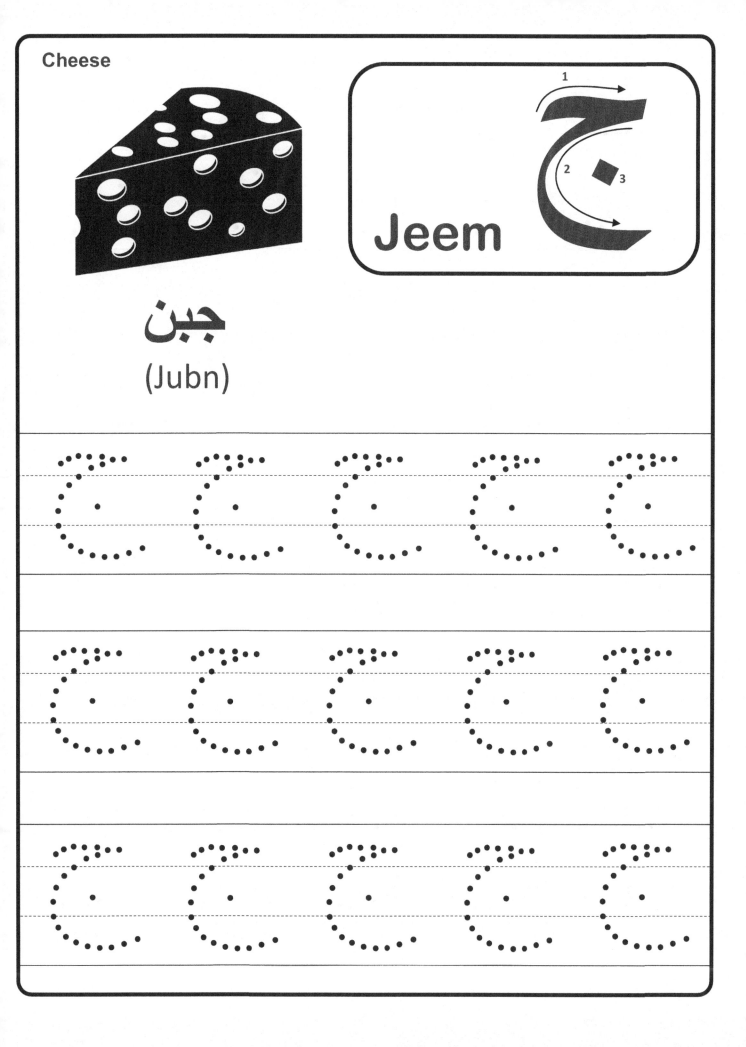

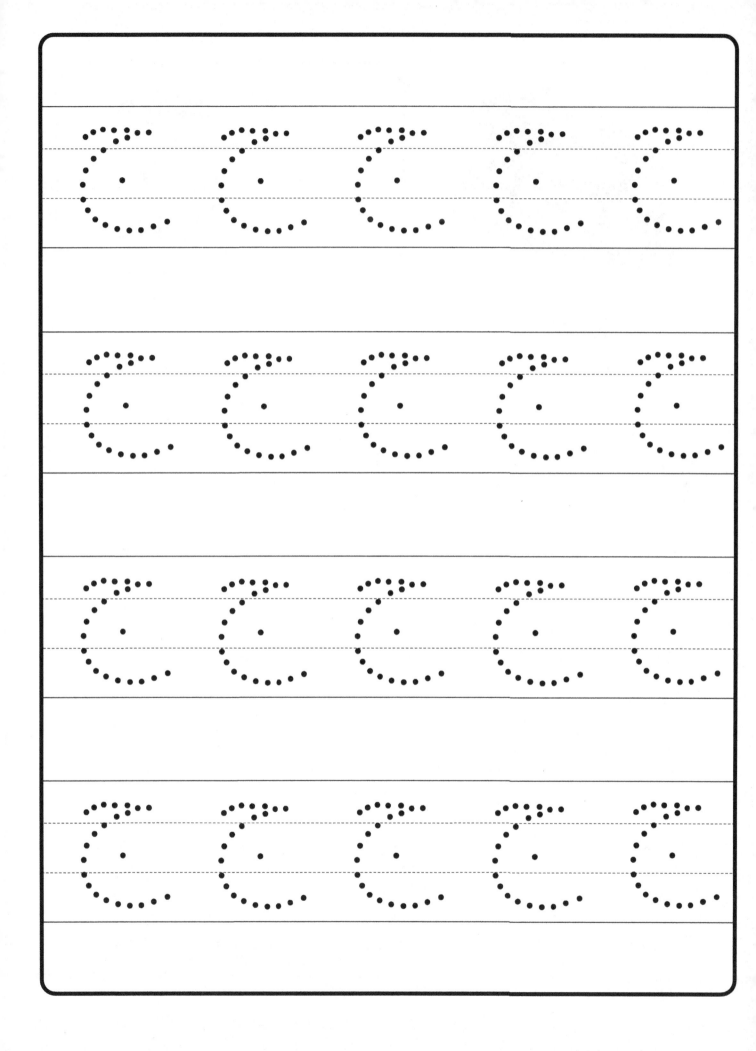

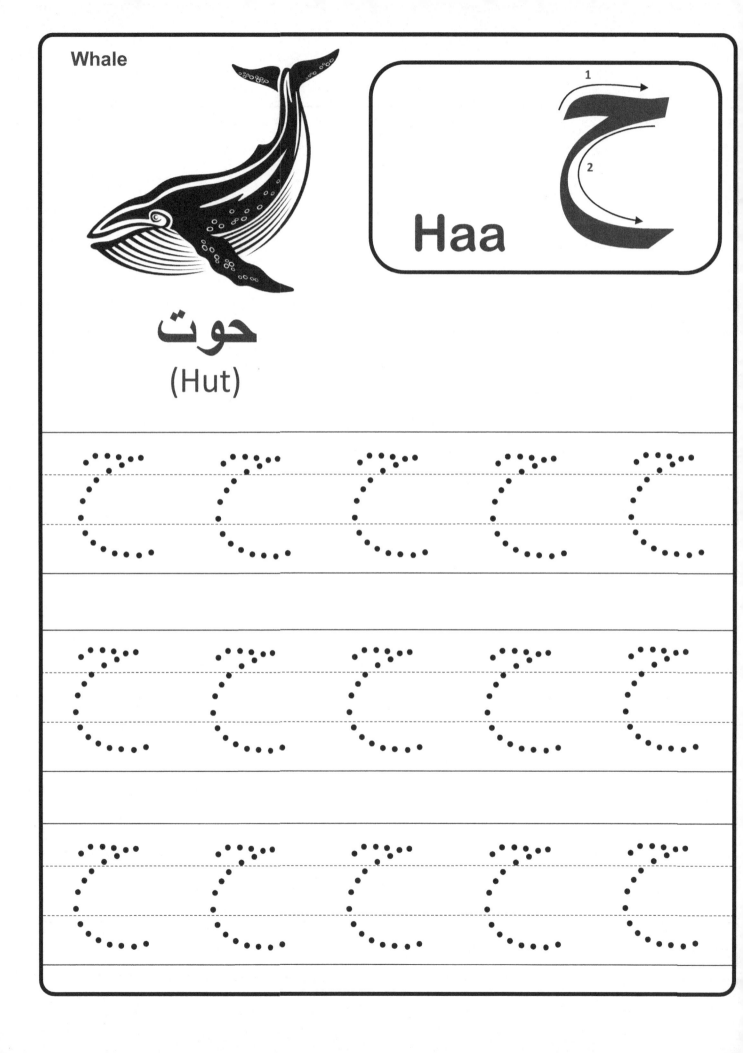

Whale

حوت

(Hut)

Haa

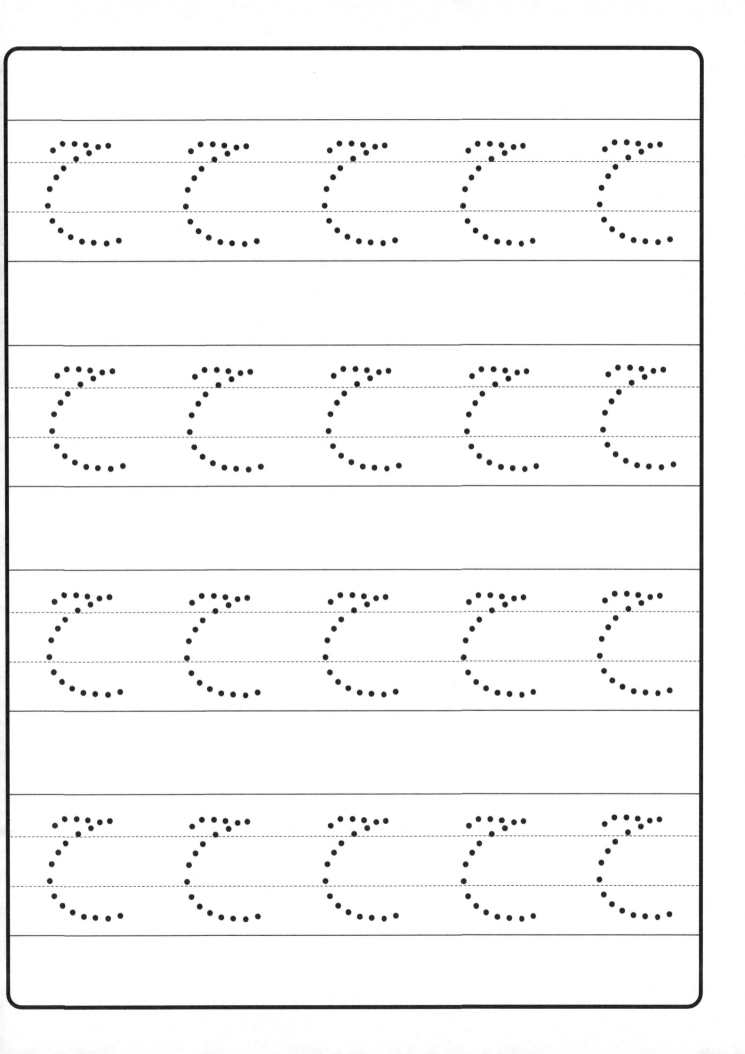

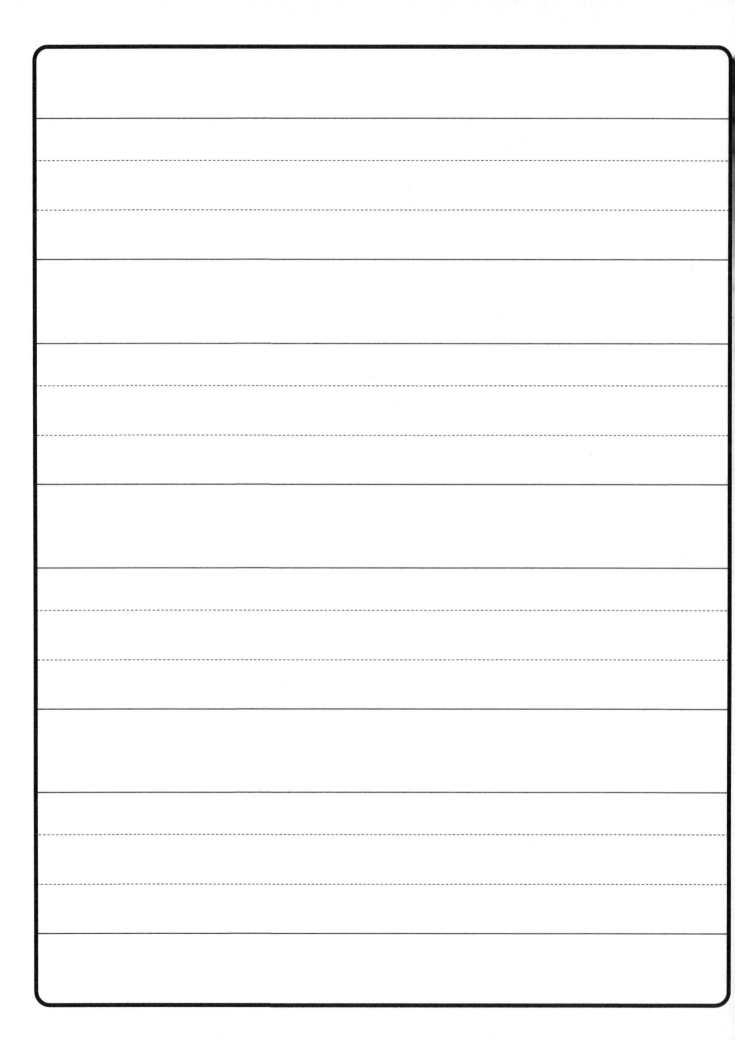

Bread

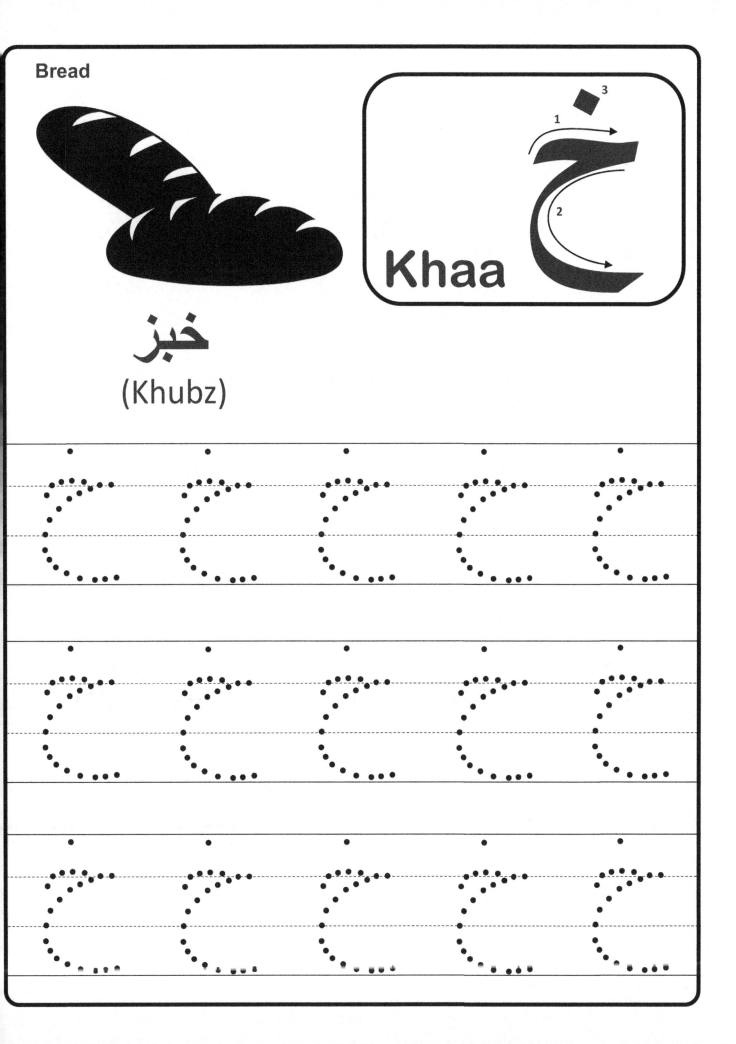

خبز

(Khubz)

Khaa

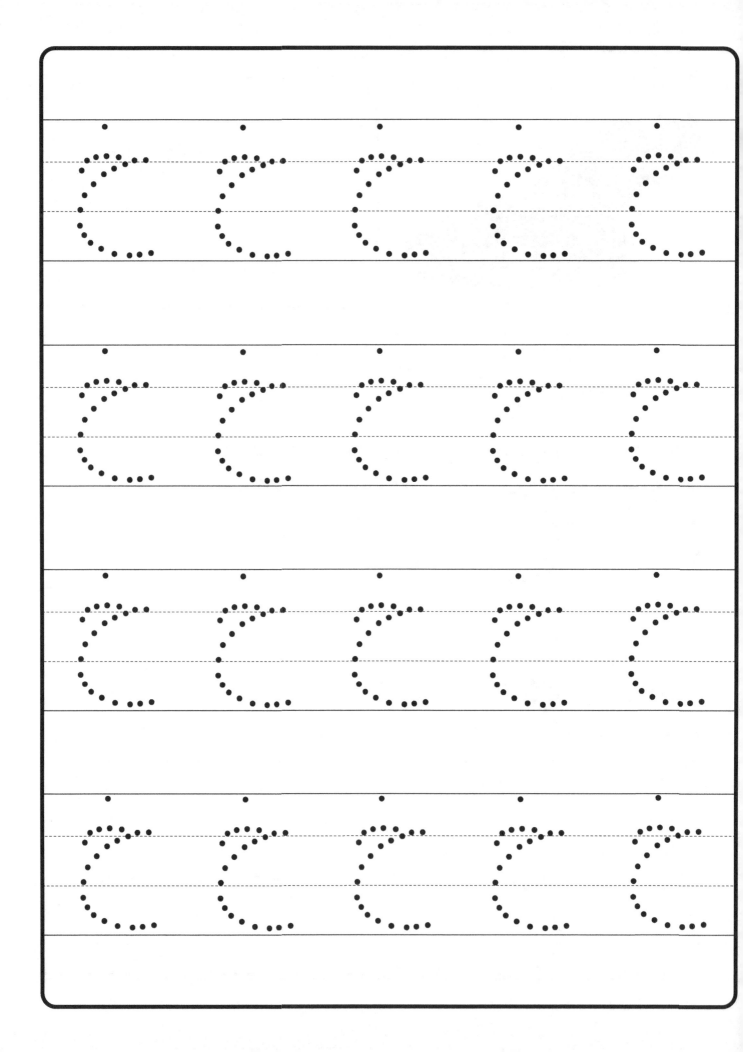

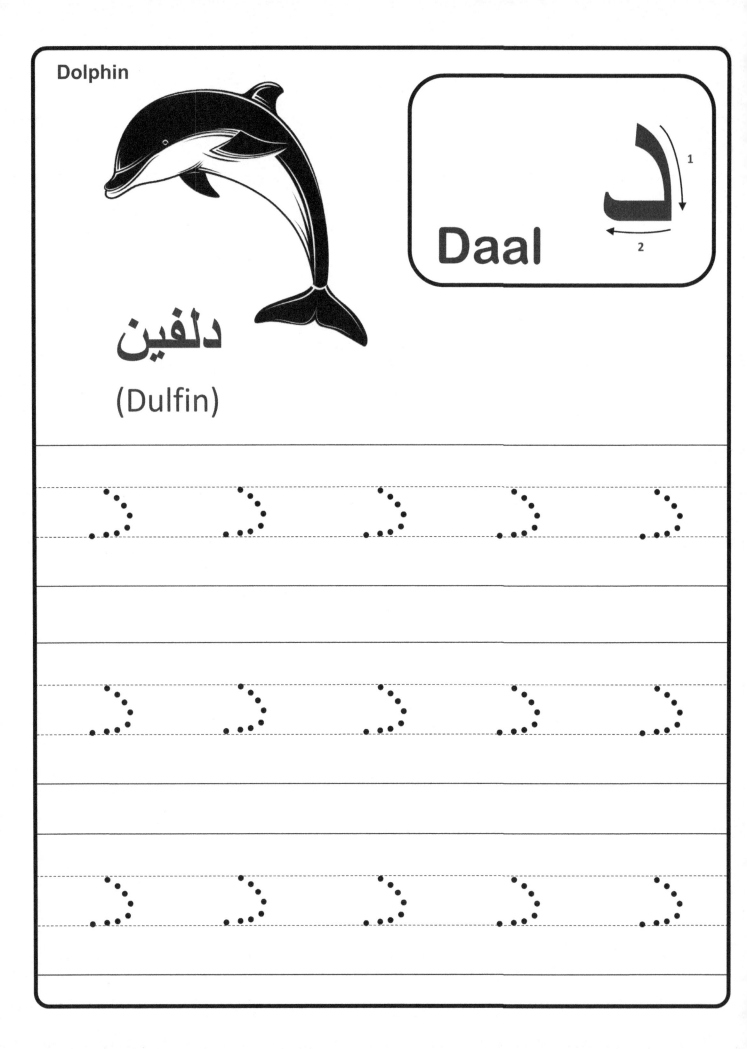

Dolphin

Daal

دلفين

(Dulfin)

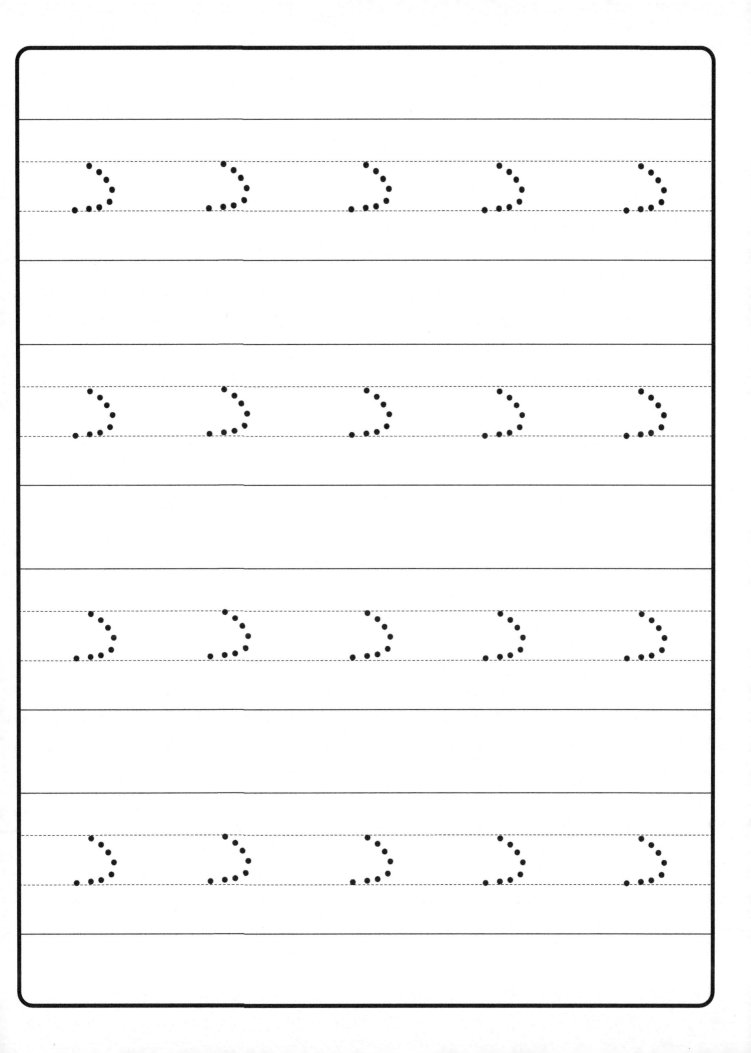

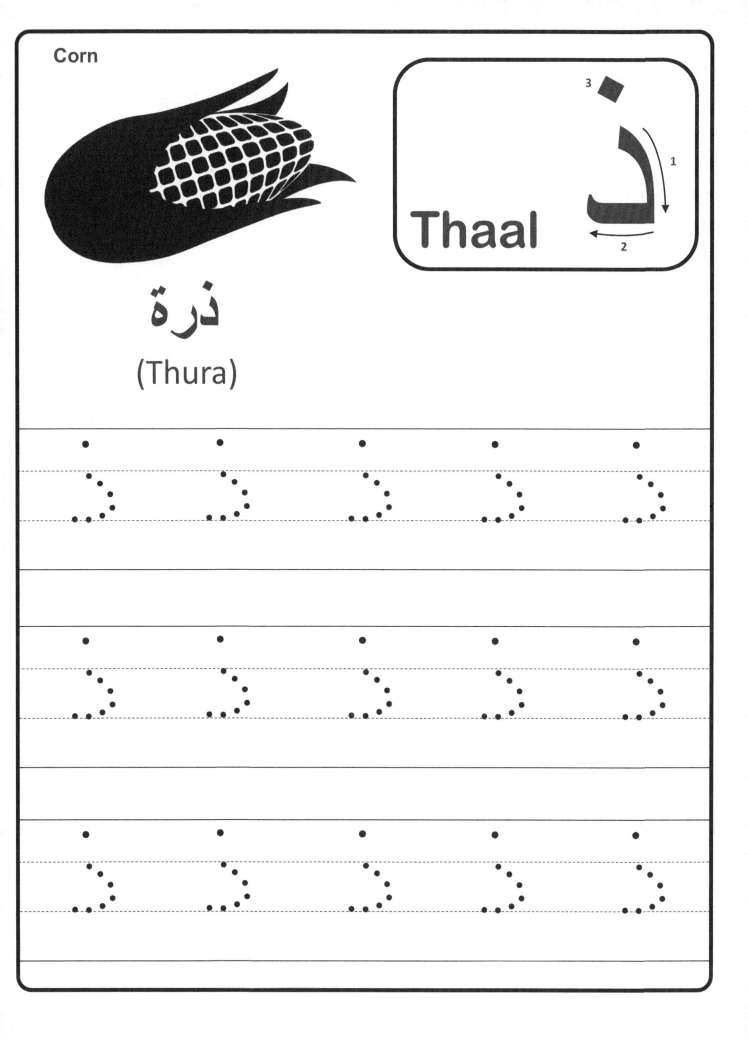

Corn

ذرة

(Thura)

Thaal

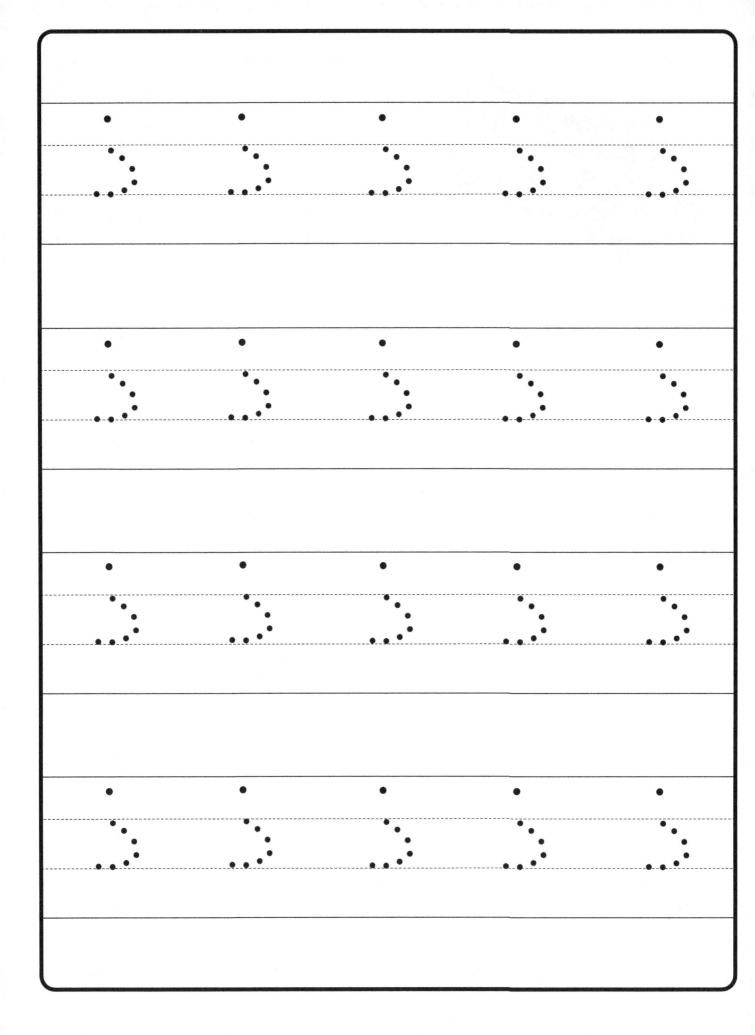

Pomegranate

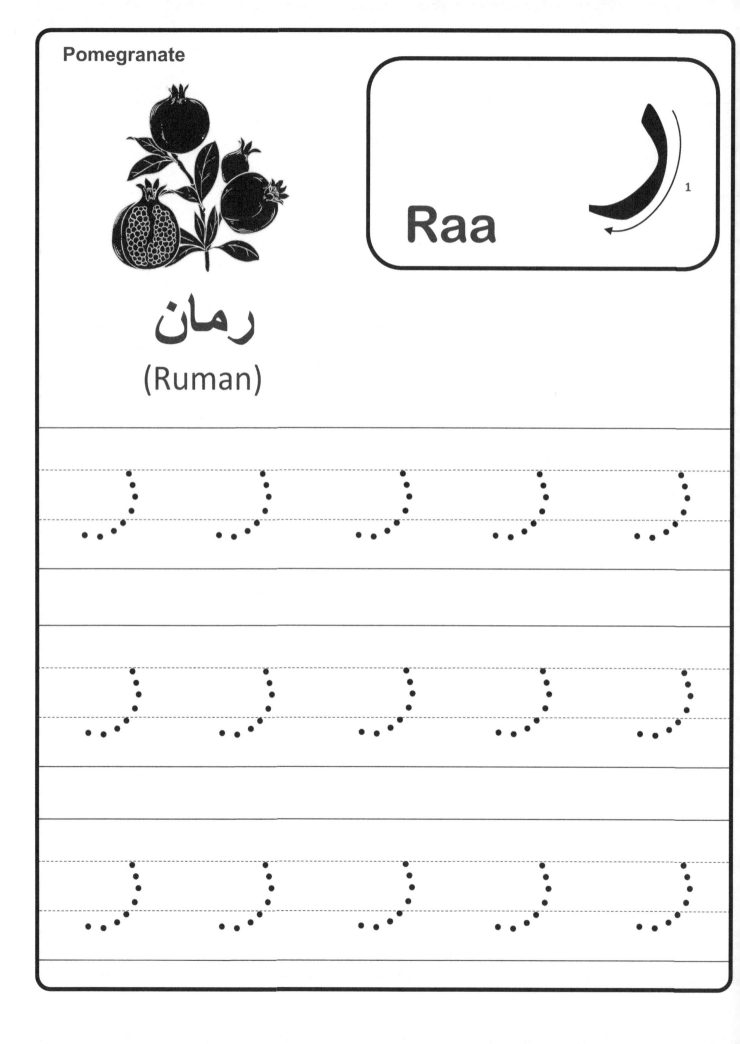

رمان

(Ruman)

Raa

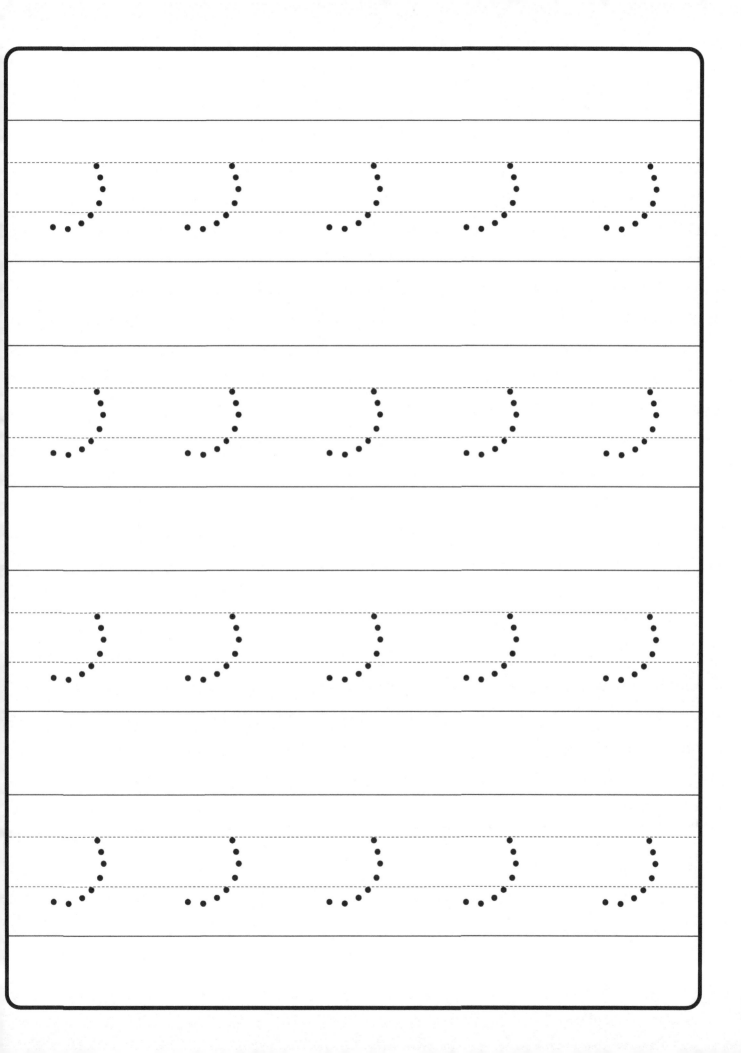

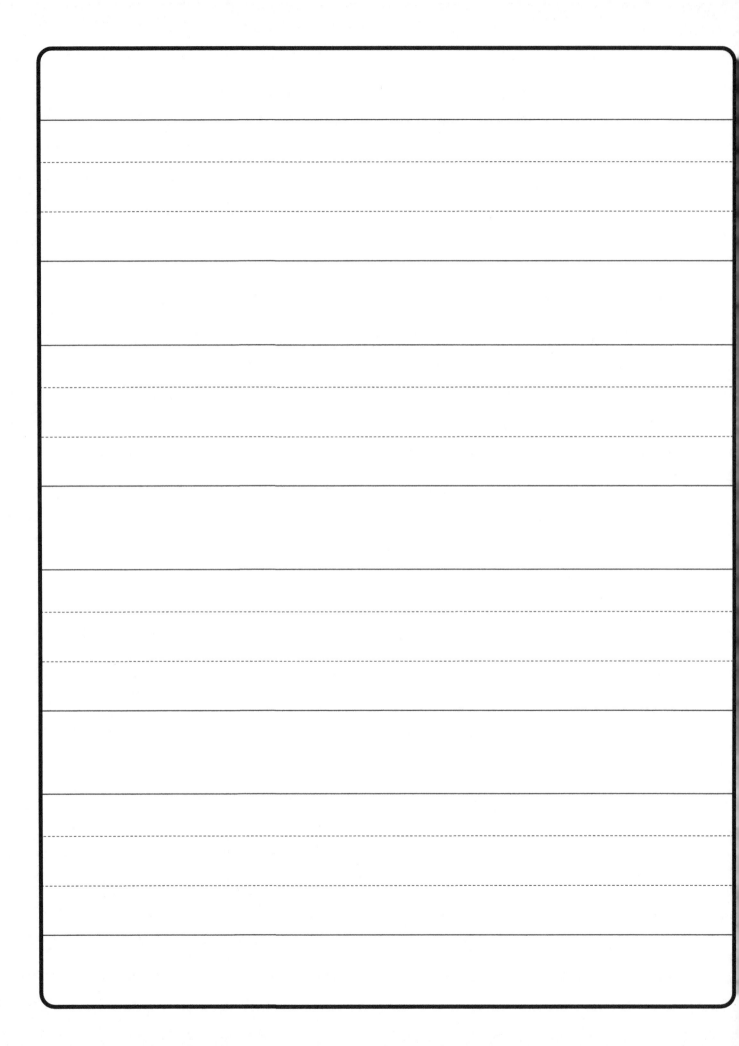

Flower

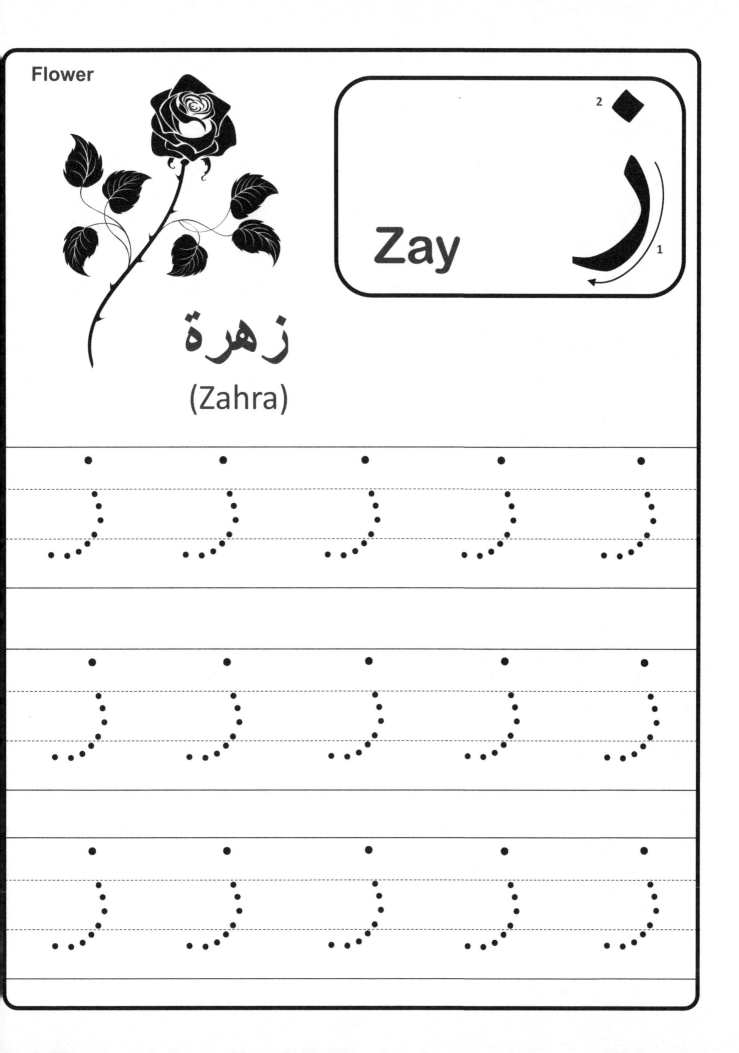

زهرة

(Zahra)

Zay

2
1

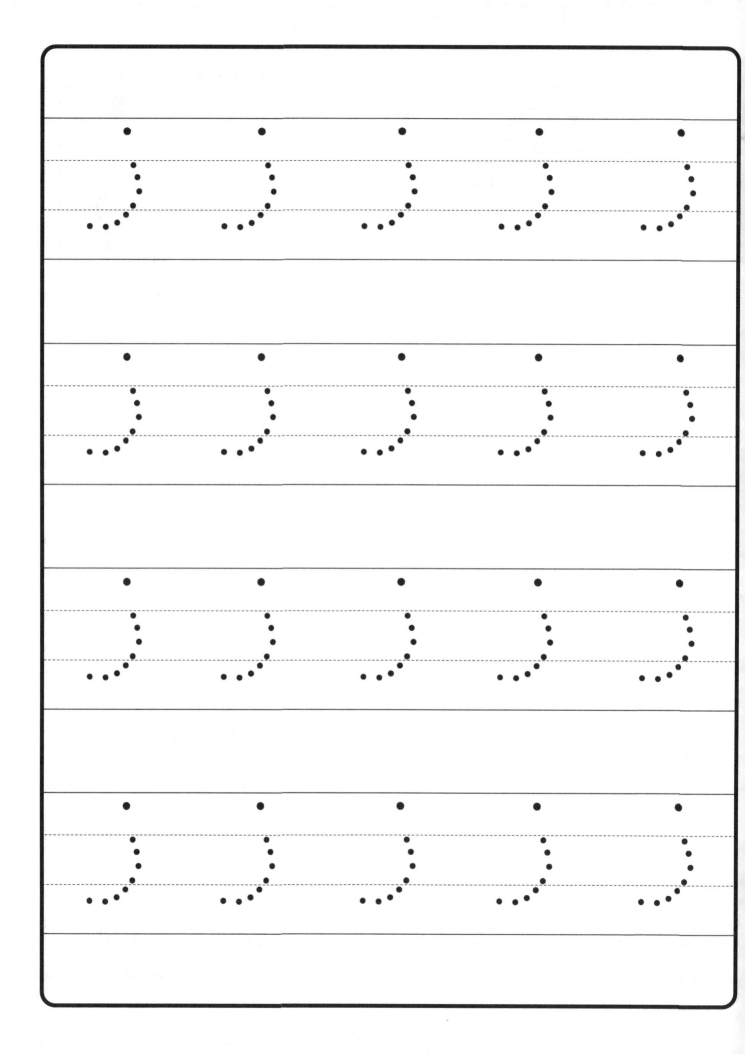

Car

Seen

 س

سيارة
(Sayara)

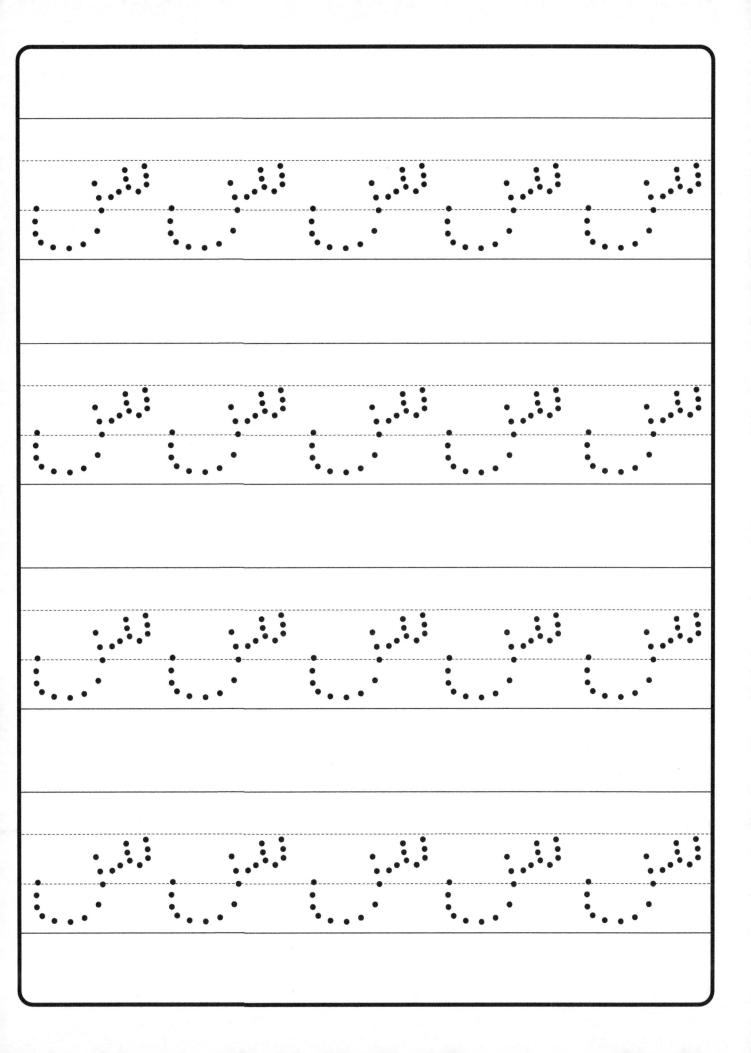

Tree

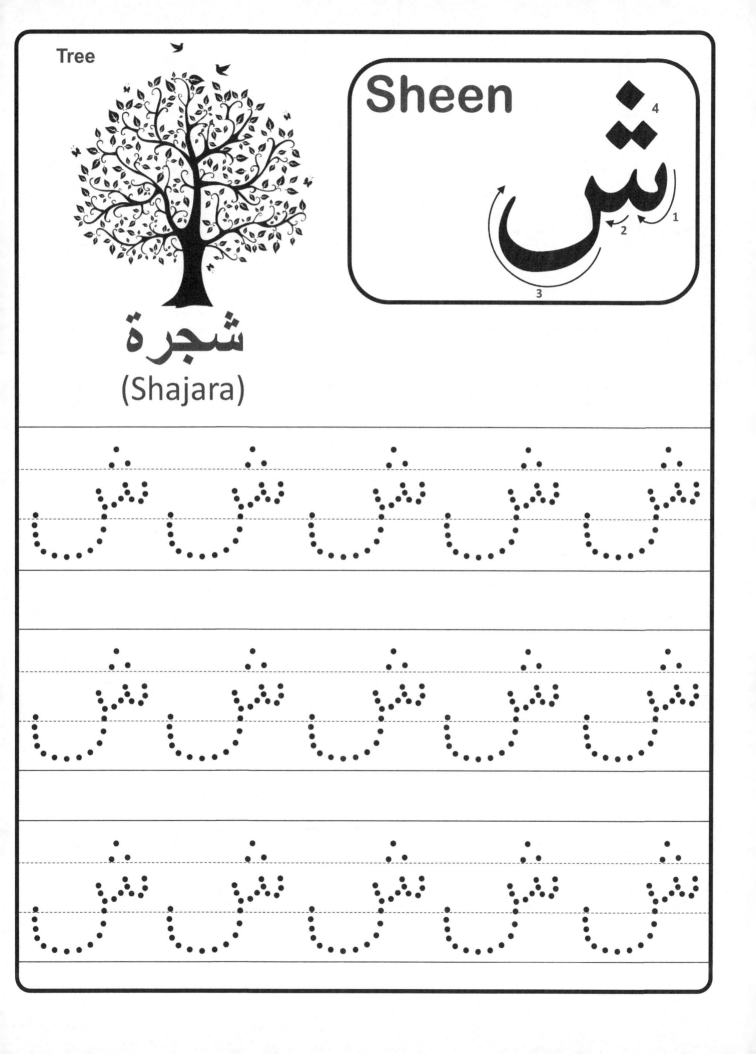

شجرة

(Shajara)

Sheen

ﺵ

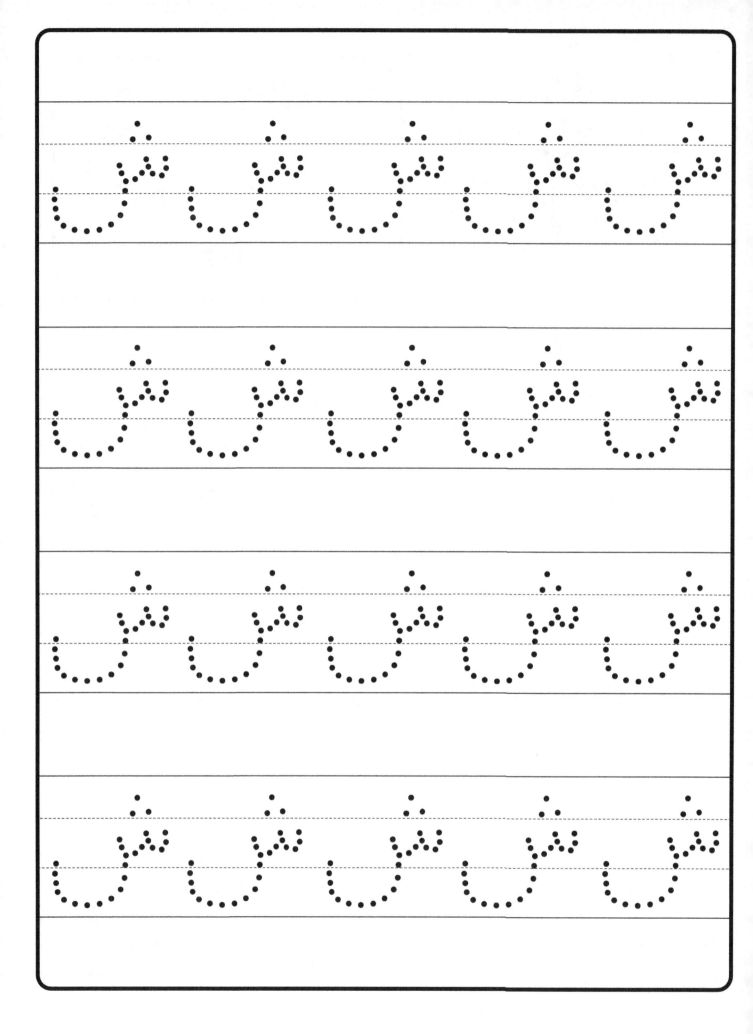

Box

صندوق

(Sunduq)

Saad

ص

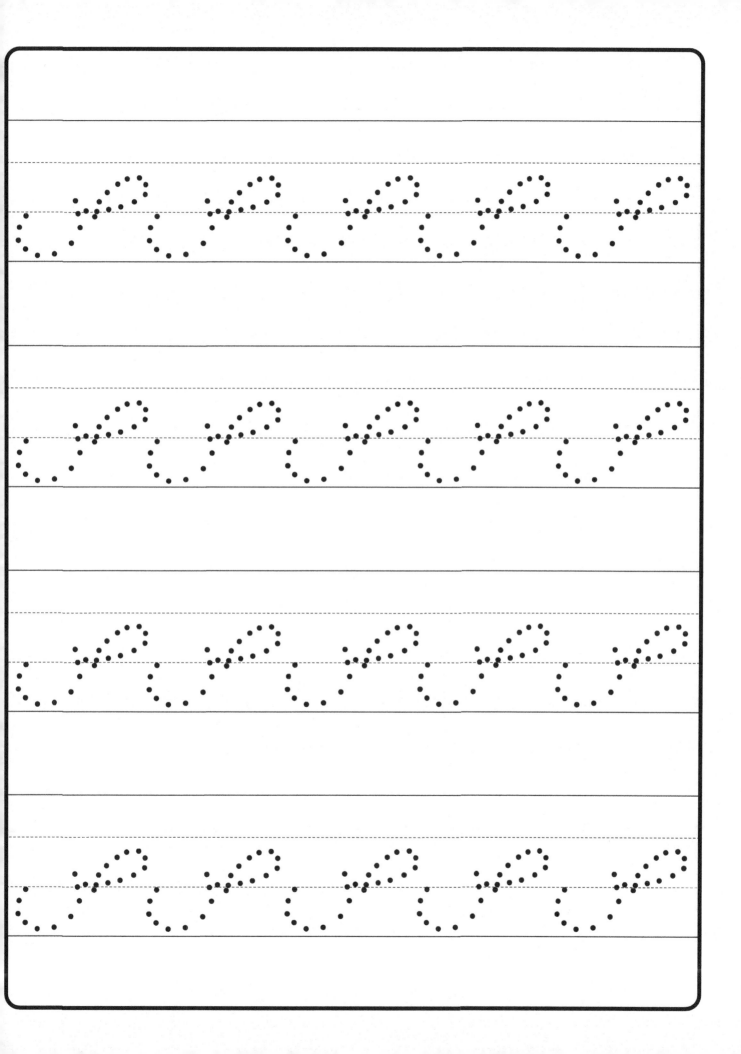

Frog

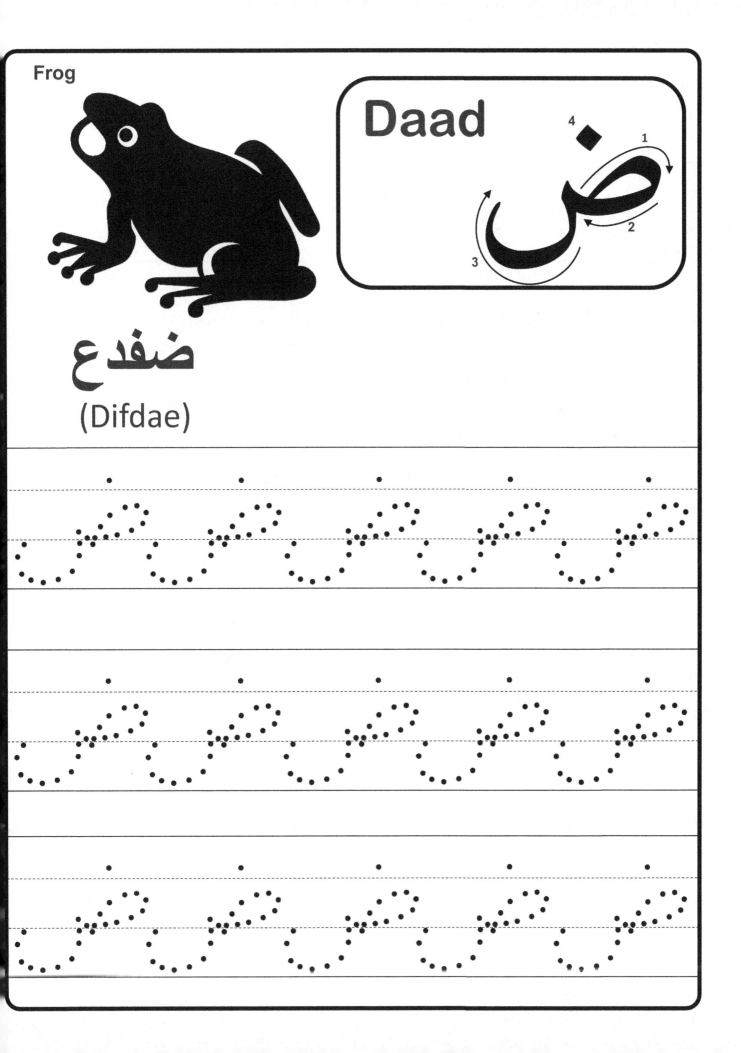

Daad

ضفدع
(Difdae)

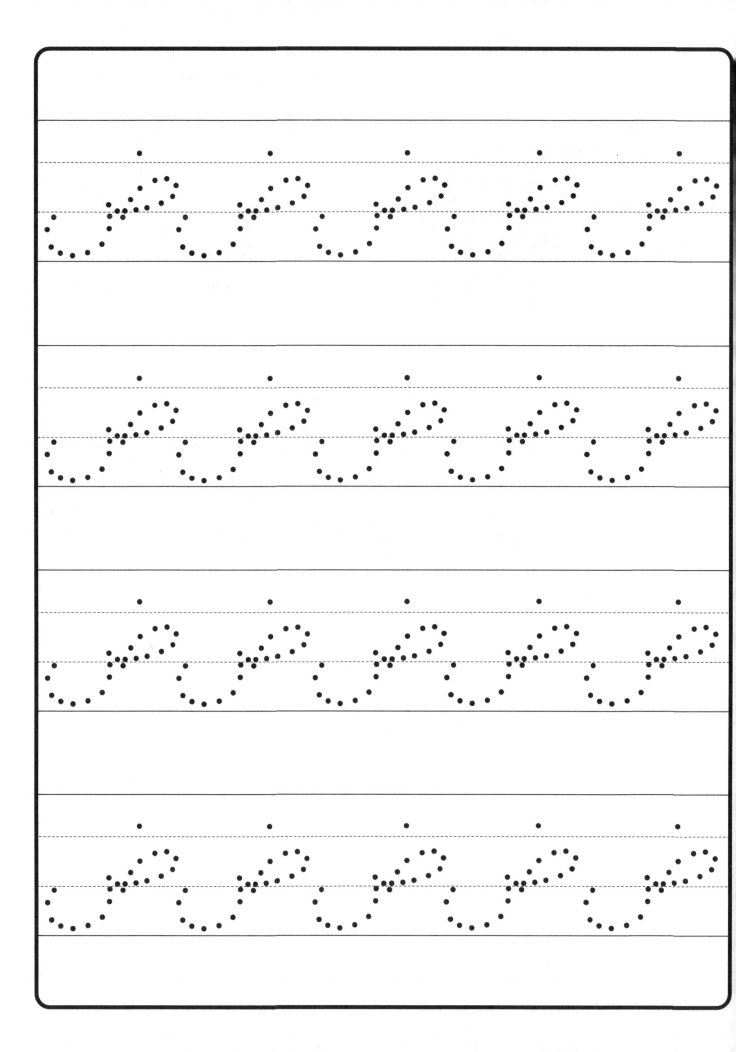

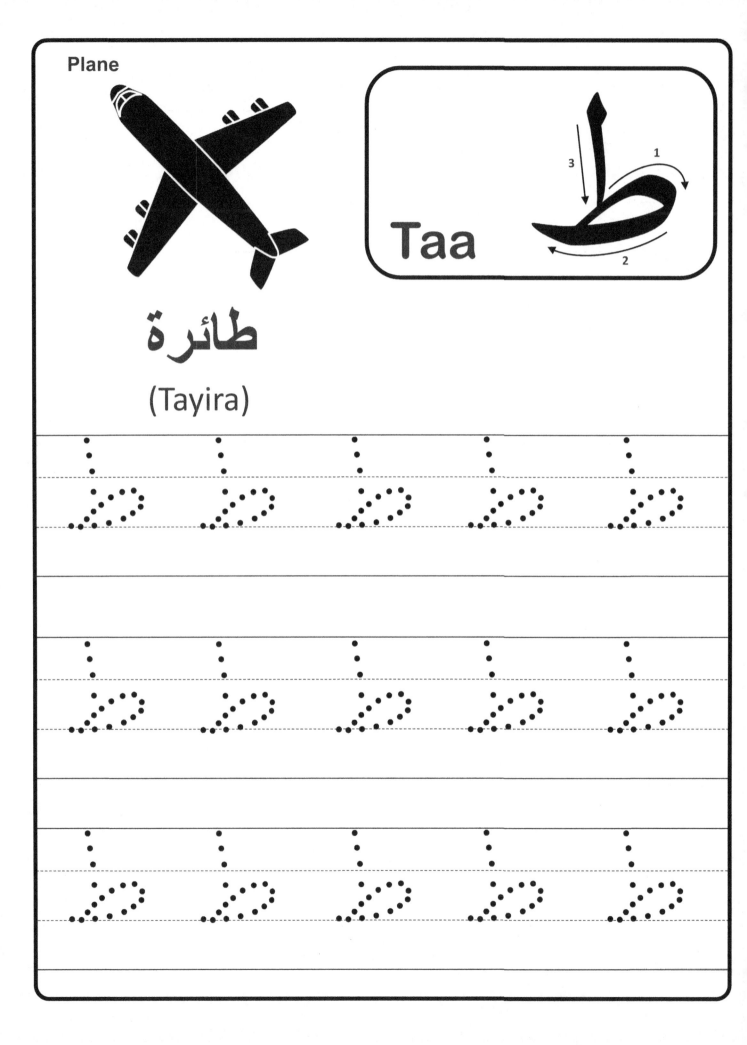

Plane

طائرة

(Tayira)

Taa

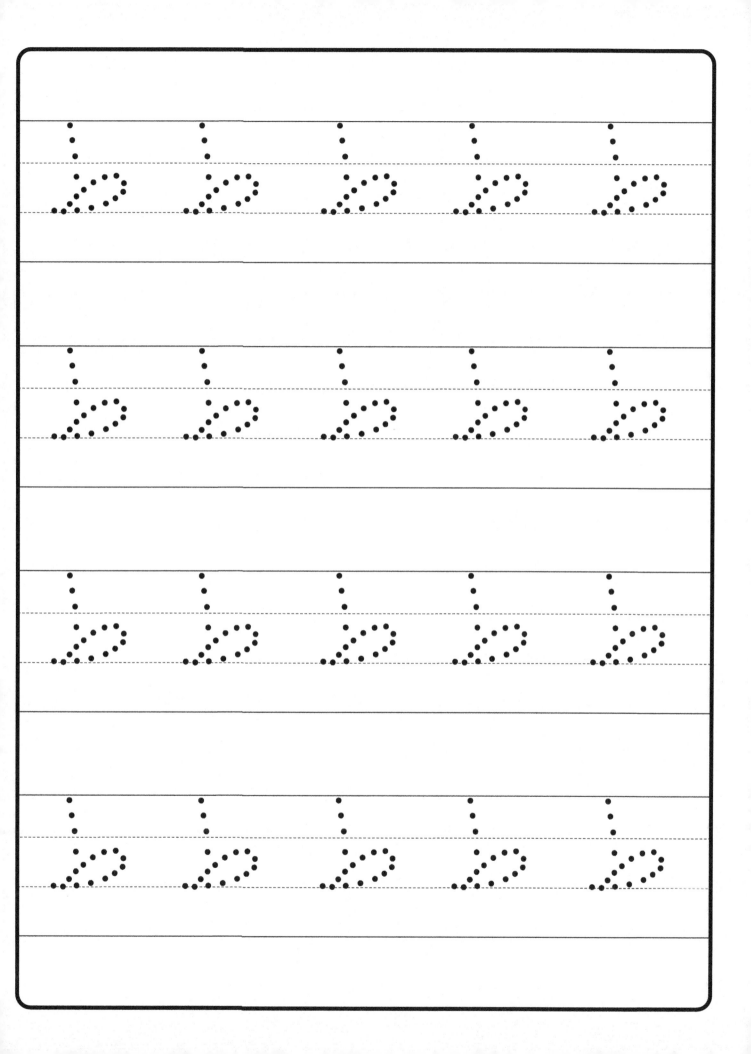

Dhaa

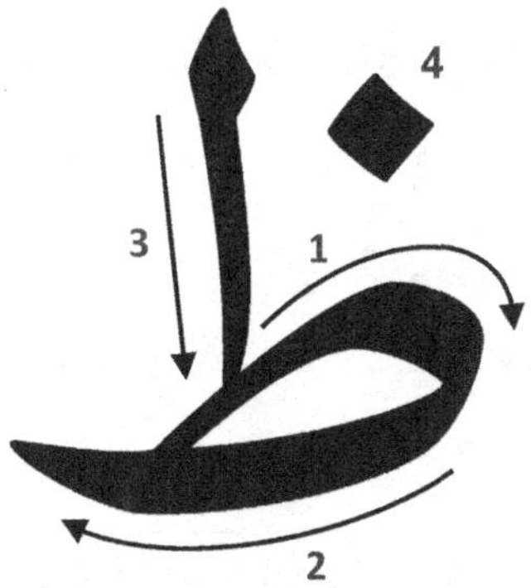

ظرف

(Dharf)

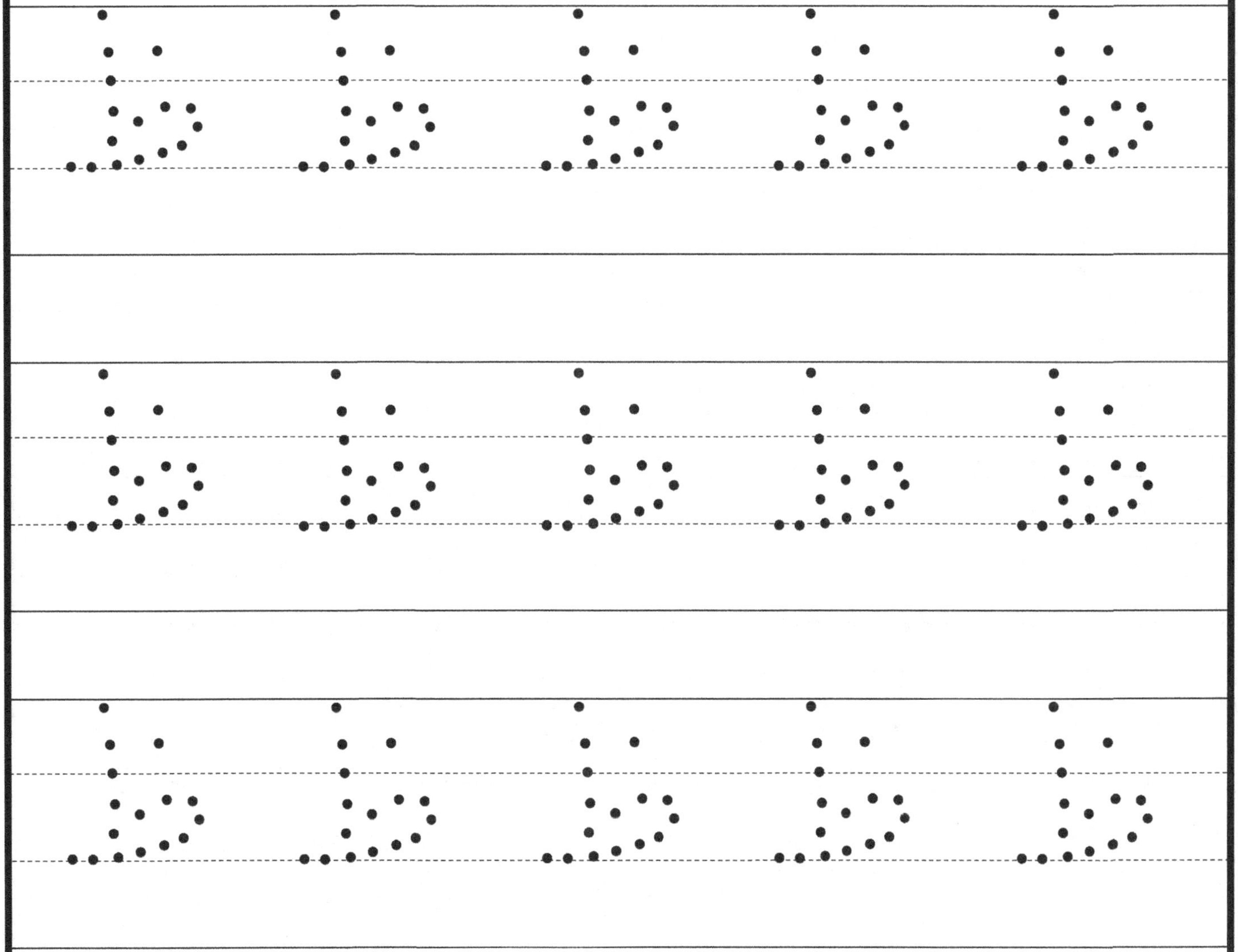

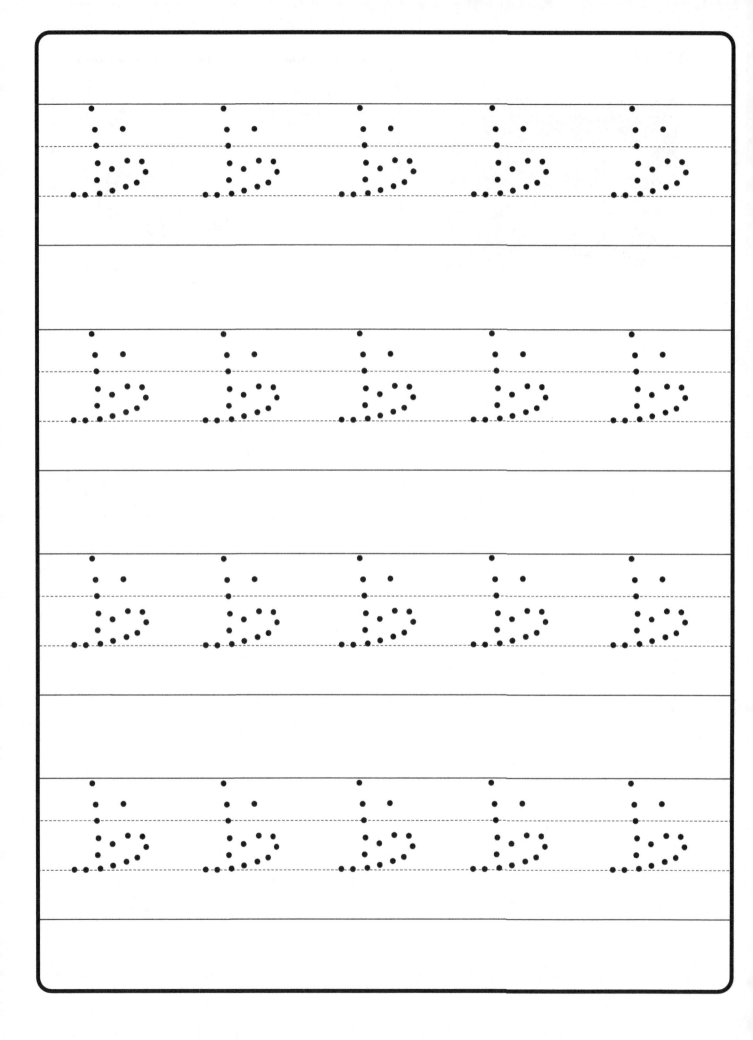

Grape

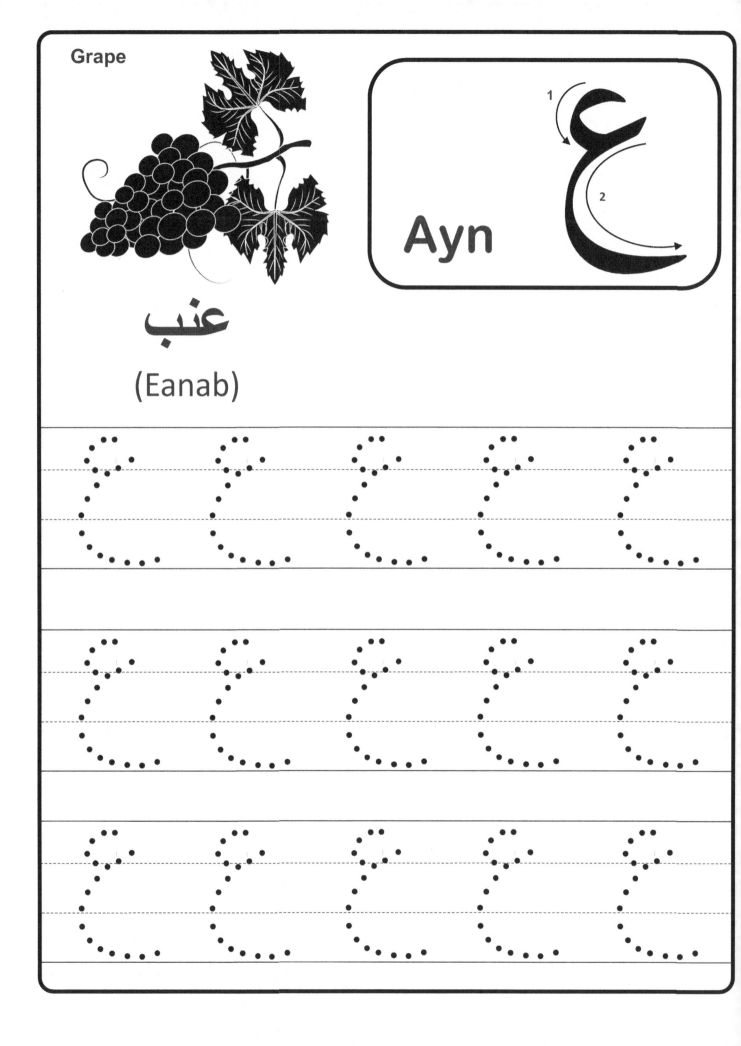

عنب

(Eanab)

Ayn

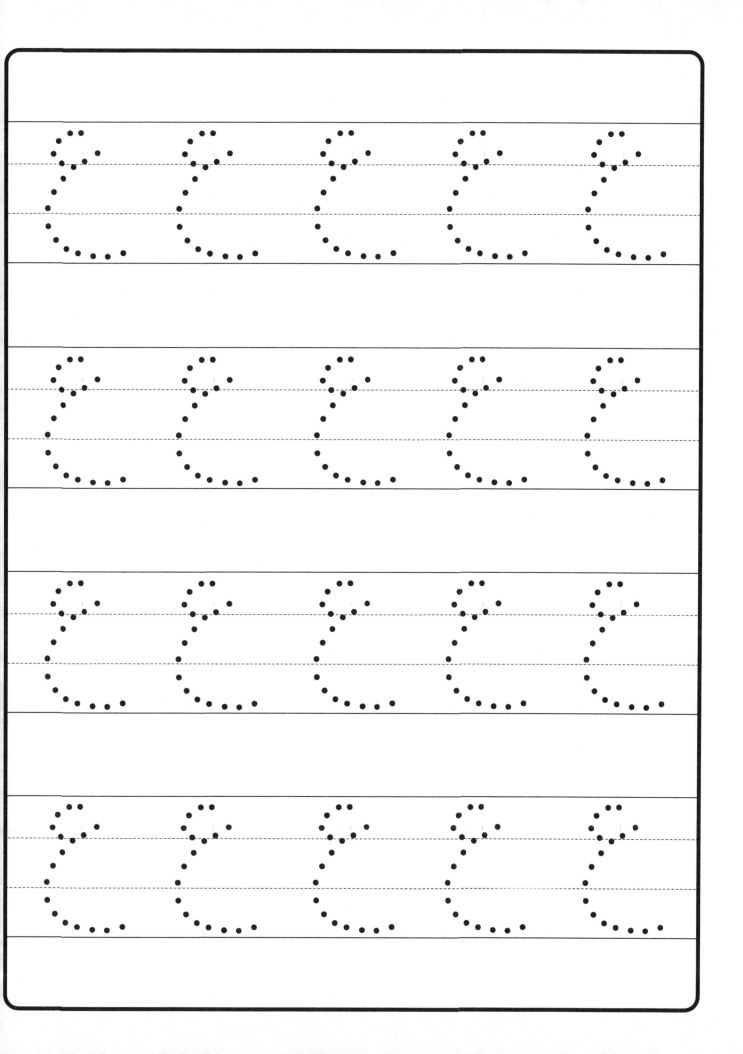

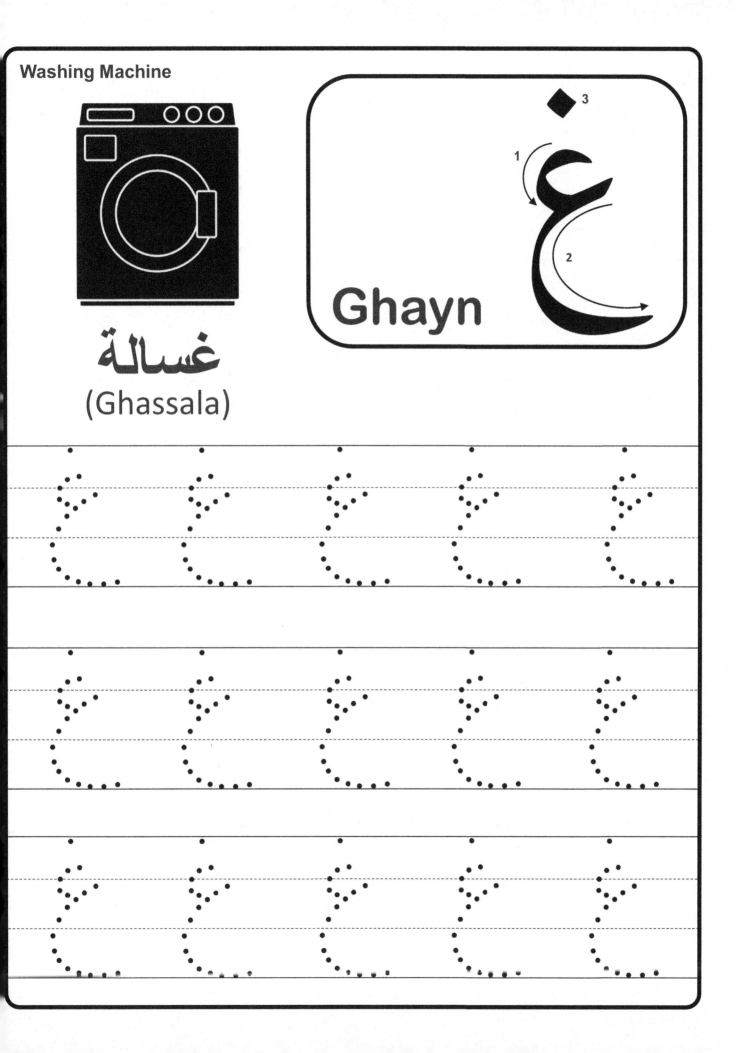

Washing Machine

غسالة

(Ghassala)

Ghayn

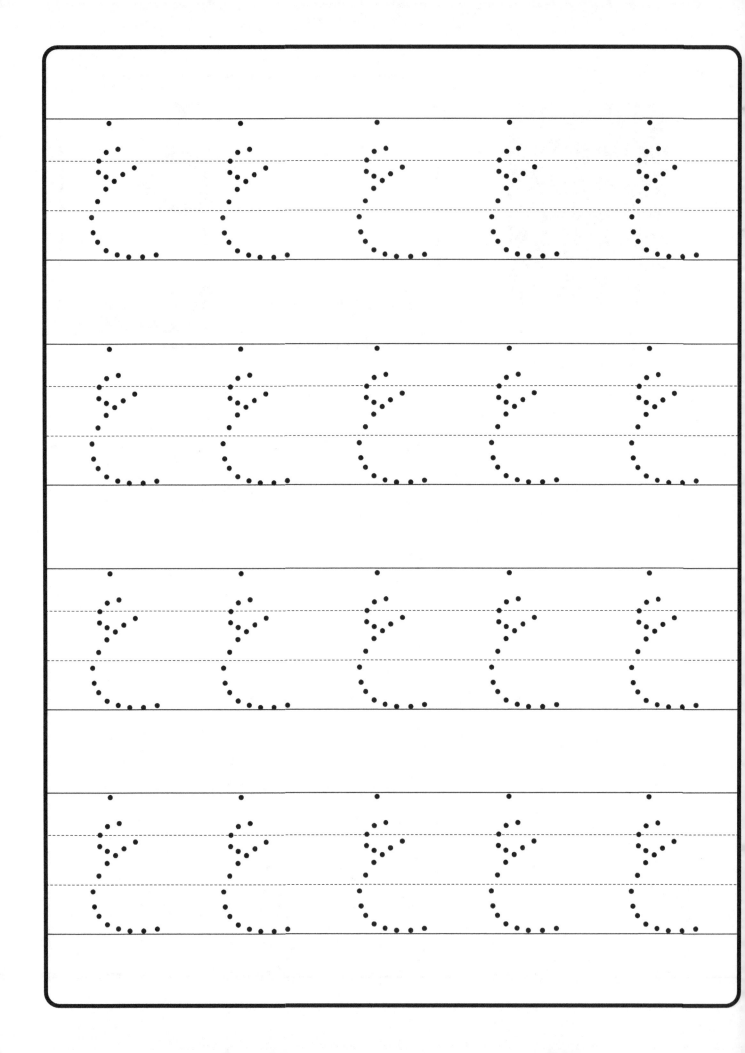

Strawberries

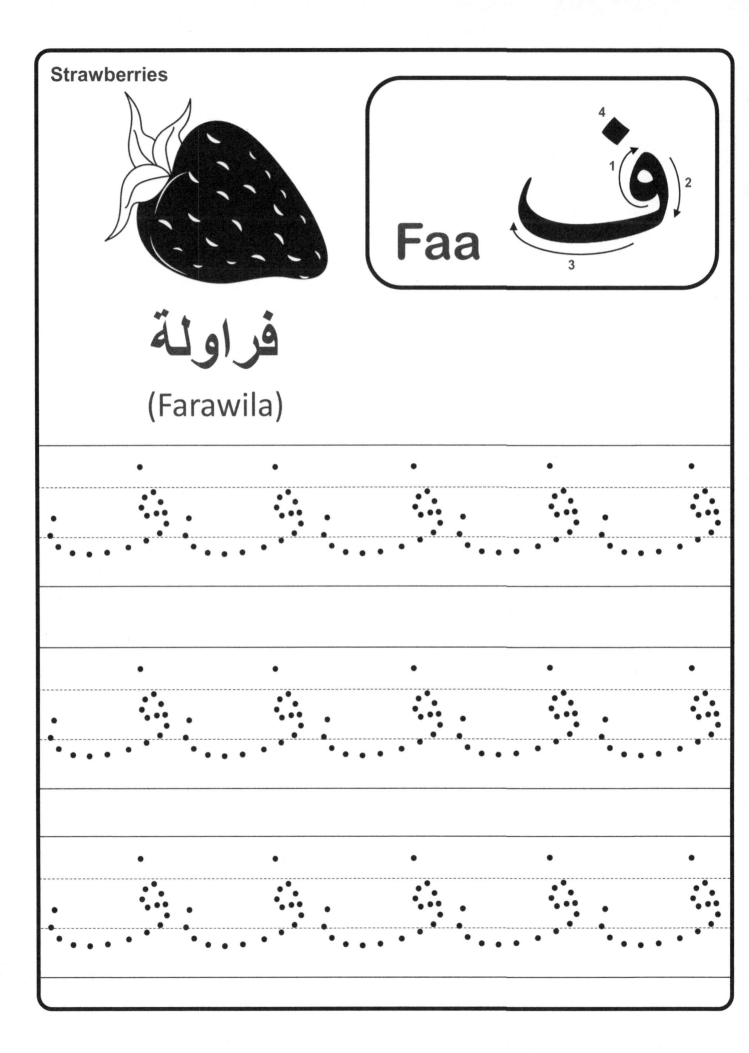

فراولة

(Farawila)

Faa

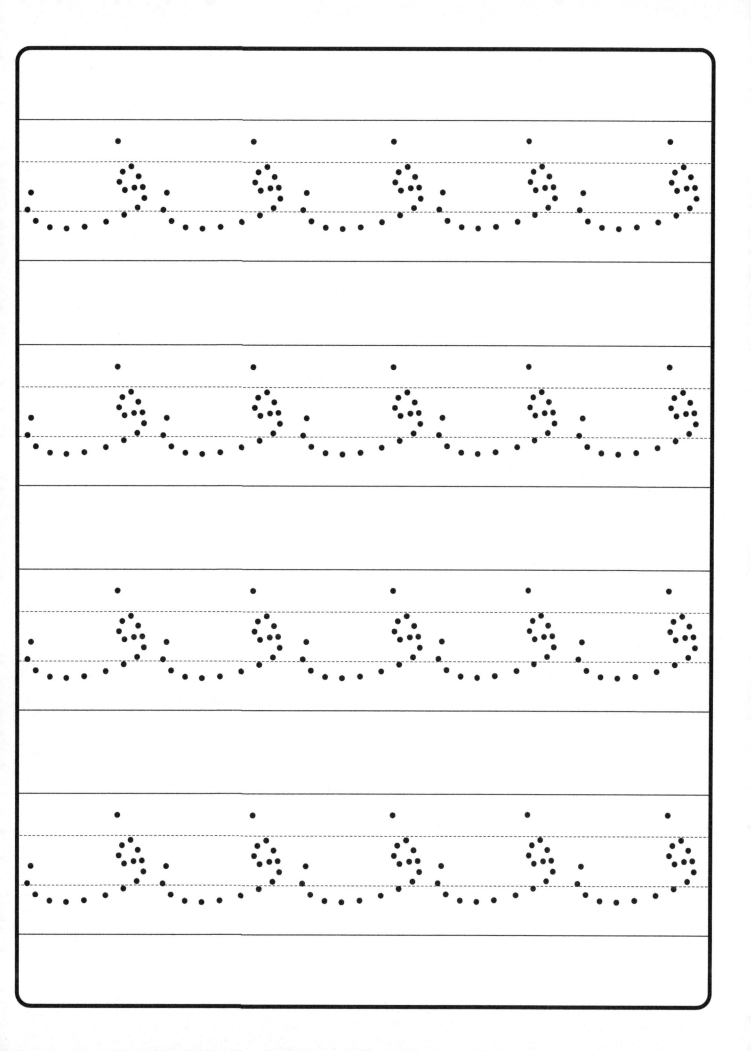

Pen

Qaaf

قلم
(Qalam)

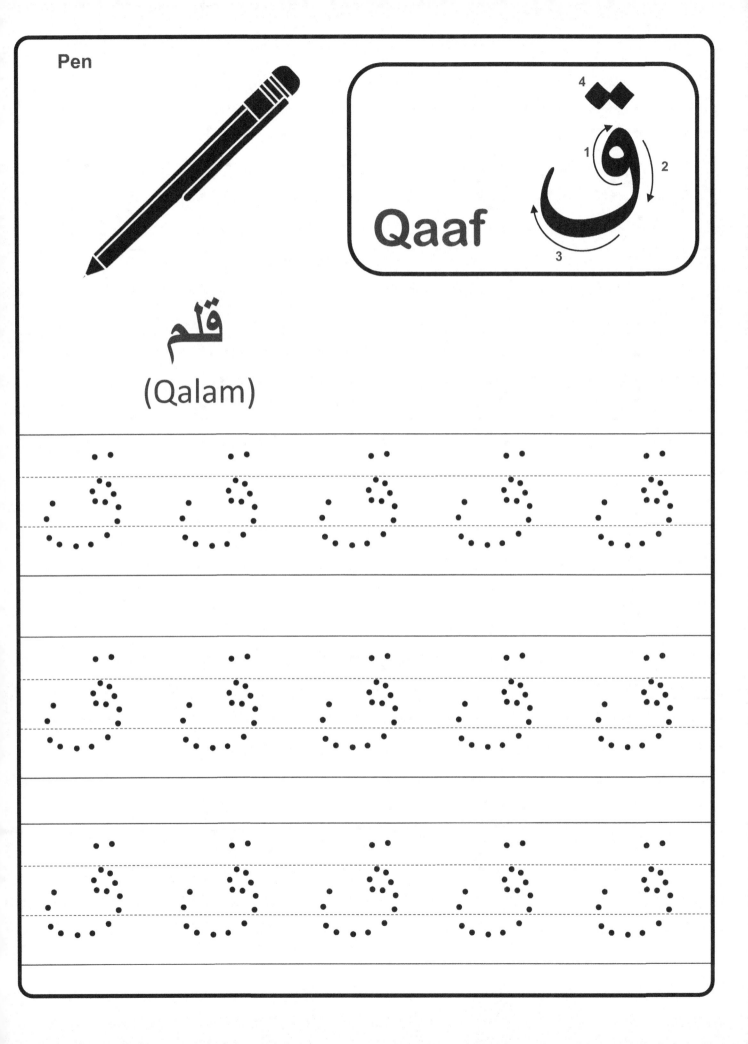

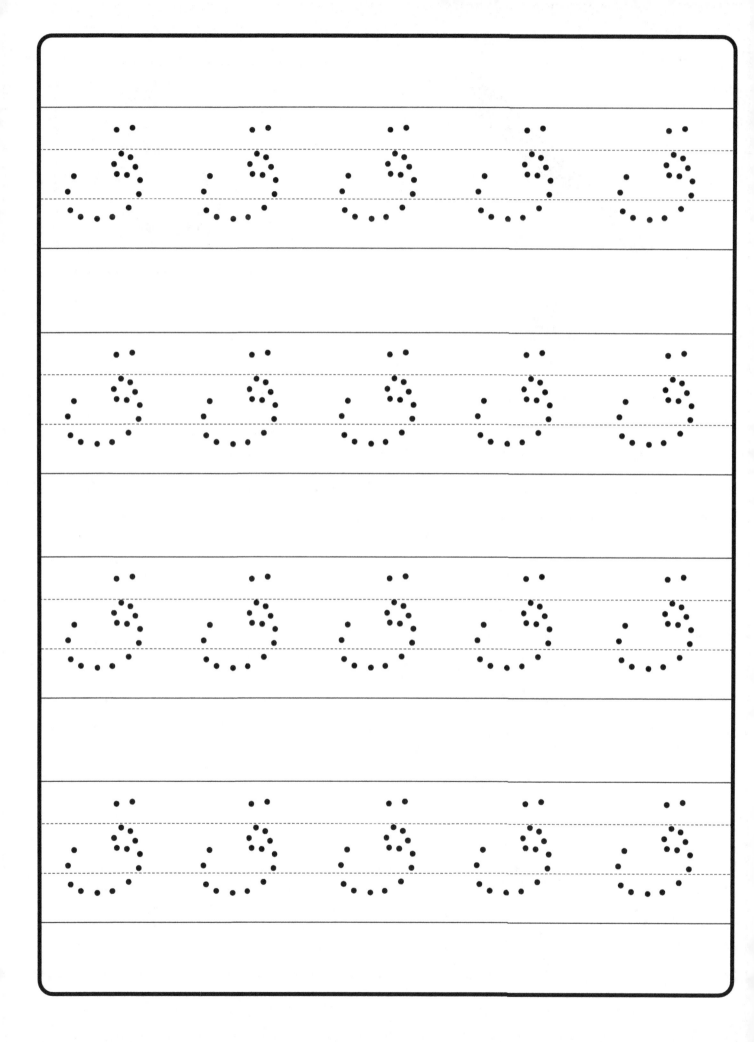

Rooster

Kaaf

ديك
(Deek)

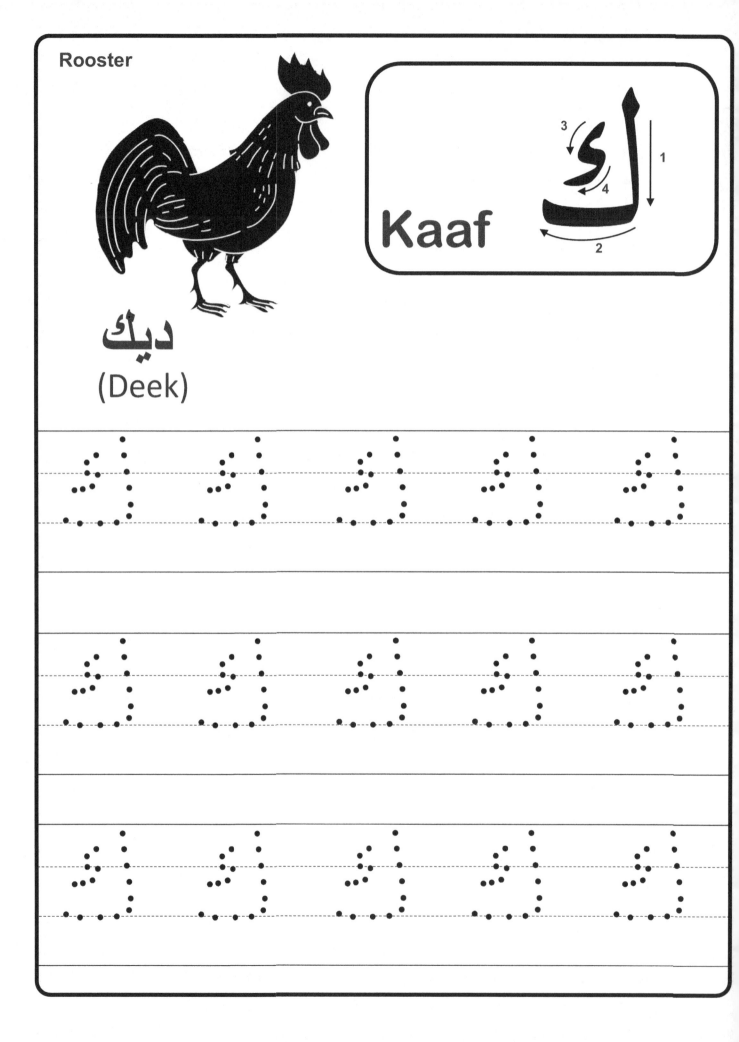

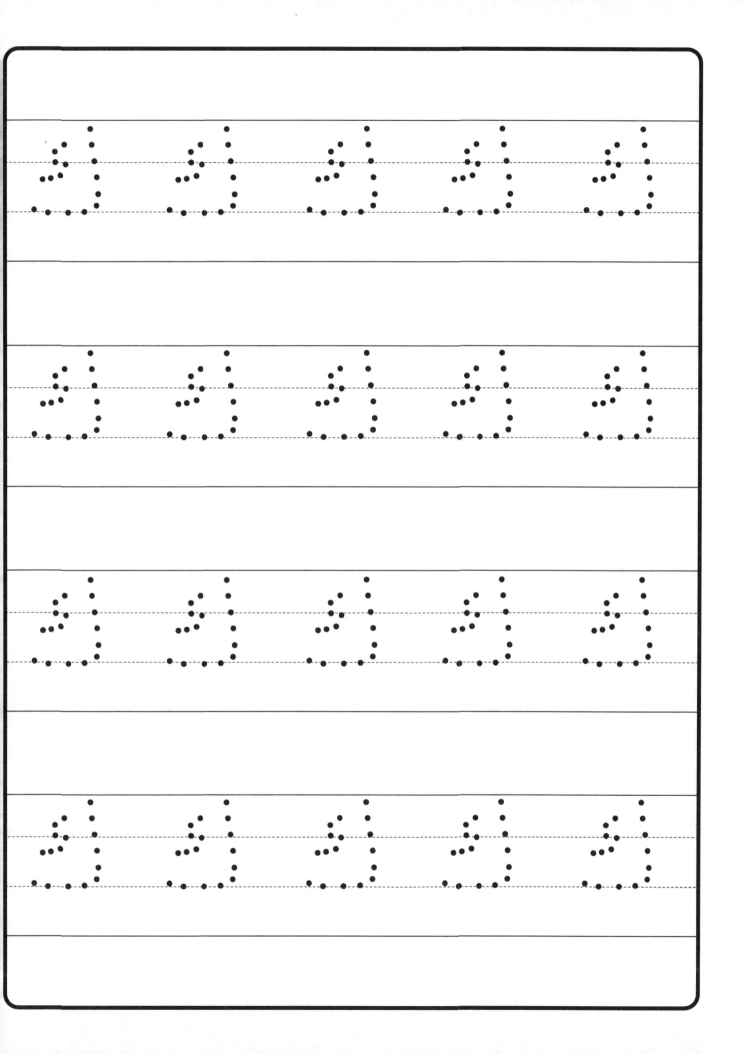

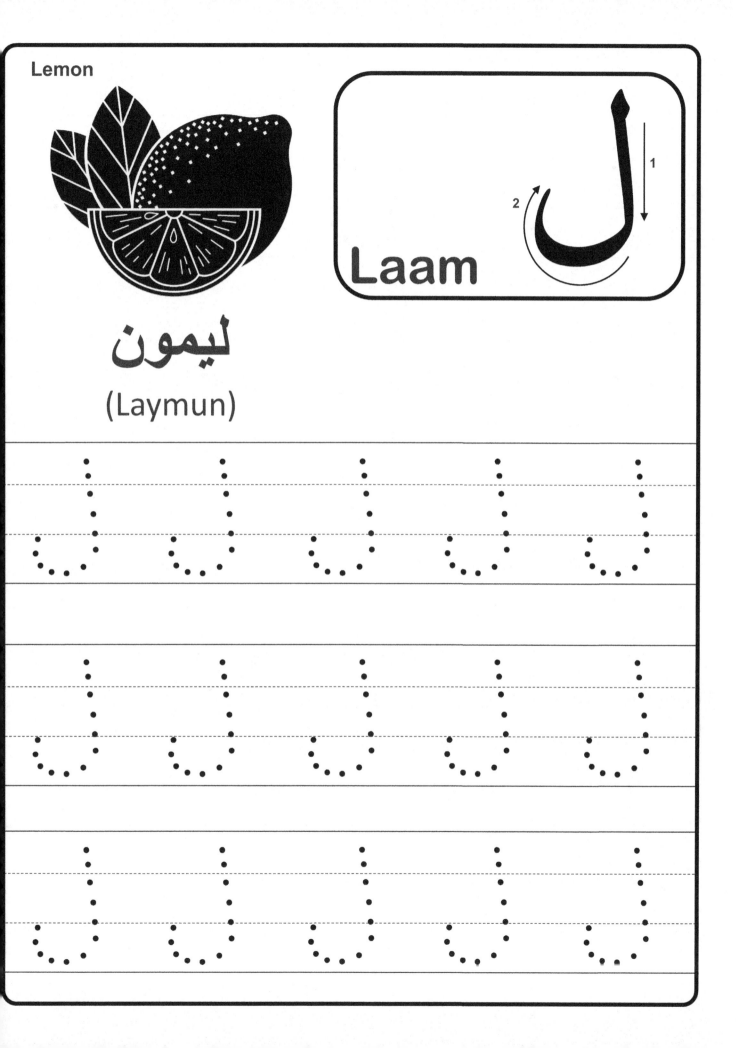

Lemon

Laam

ليمون

(Laymun)

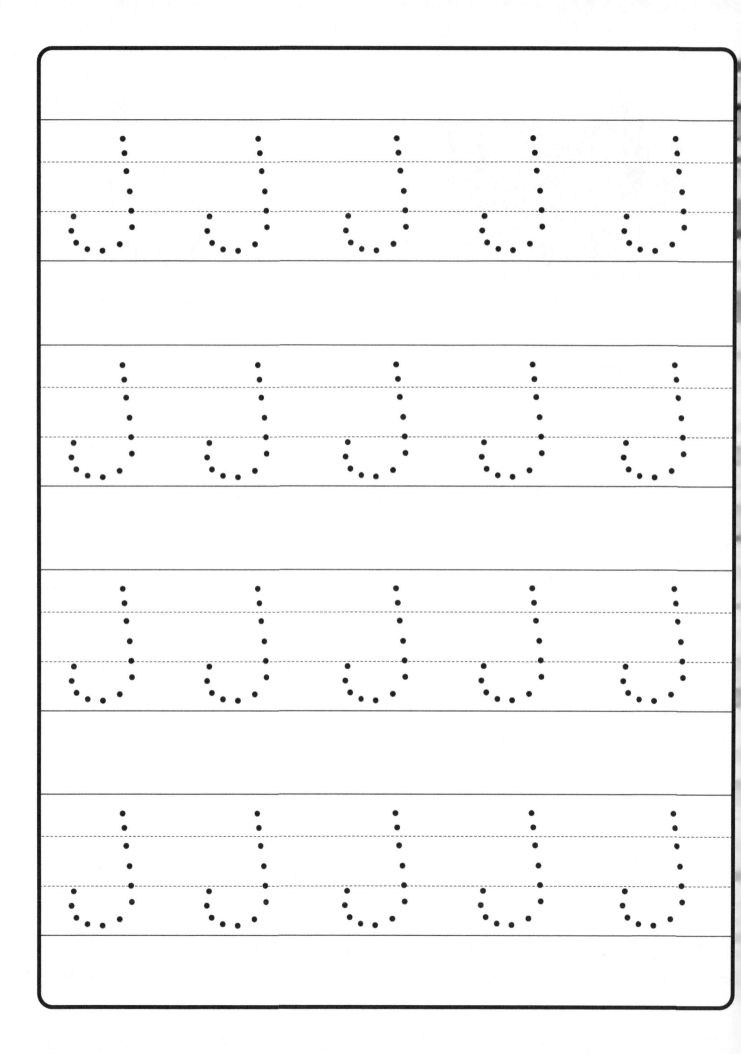

Banana

موز

(Mawz)

Meem

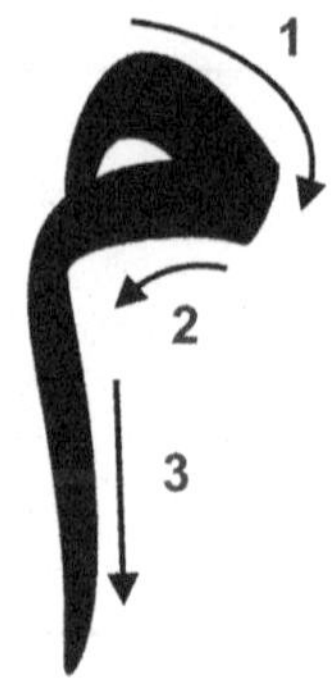

1
2
3

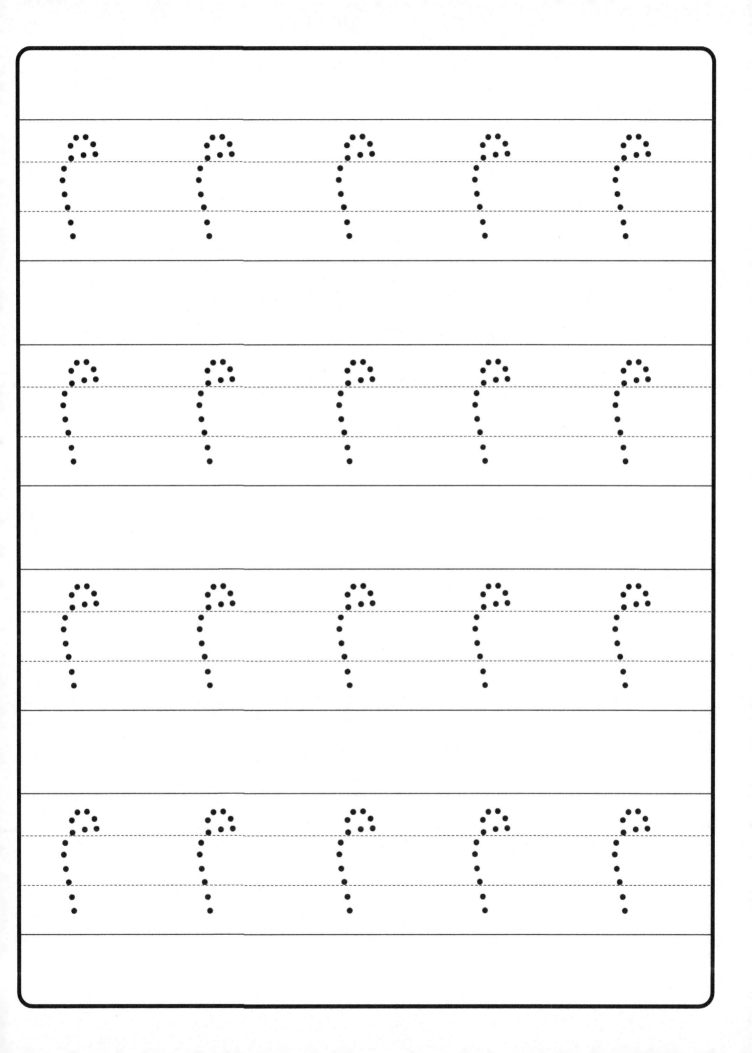

Palm

Nuun

نخلة

(Nakhla)

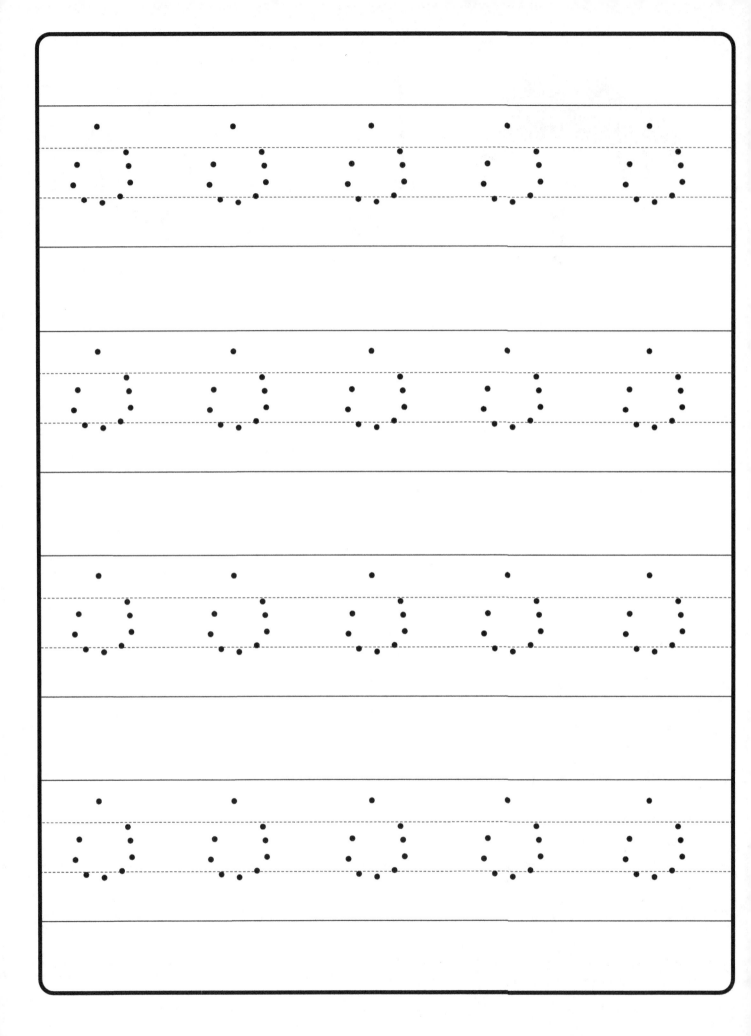

Phone

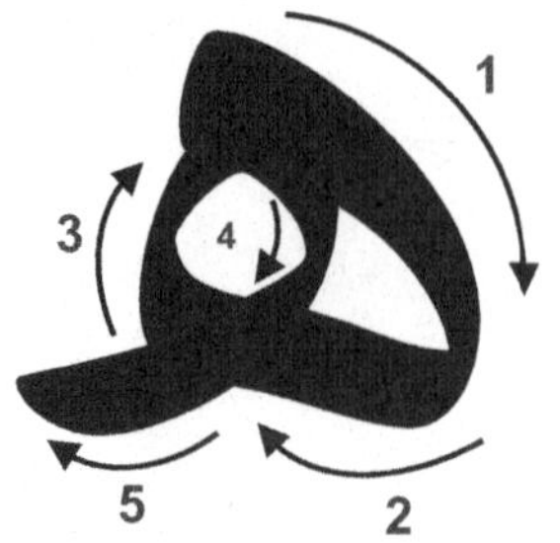

هاتف

(Hatif)

Haa

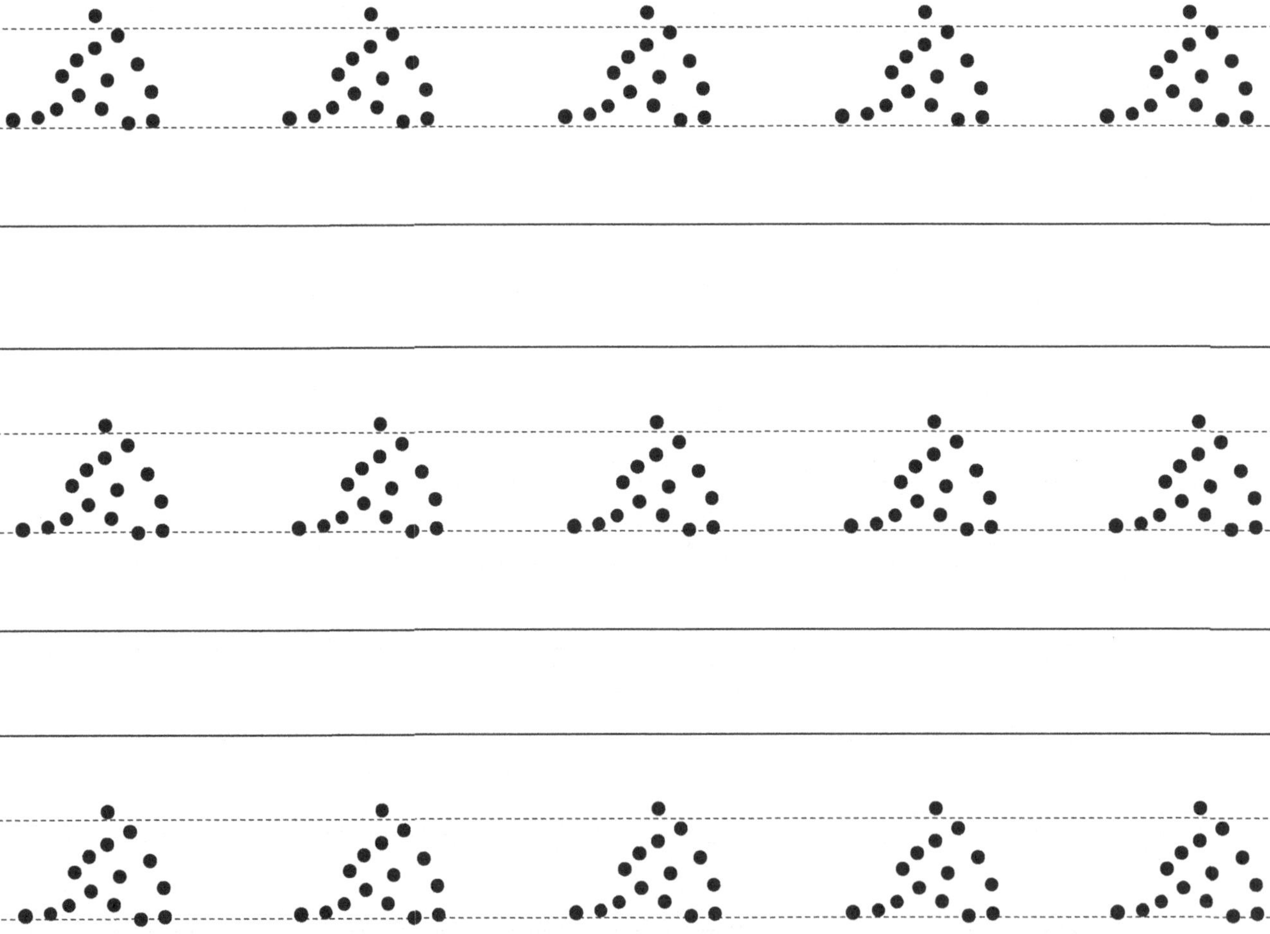

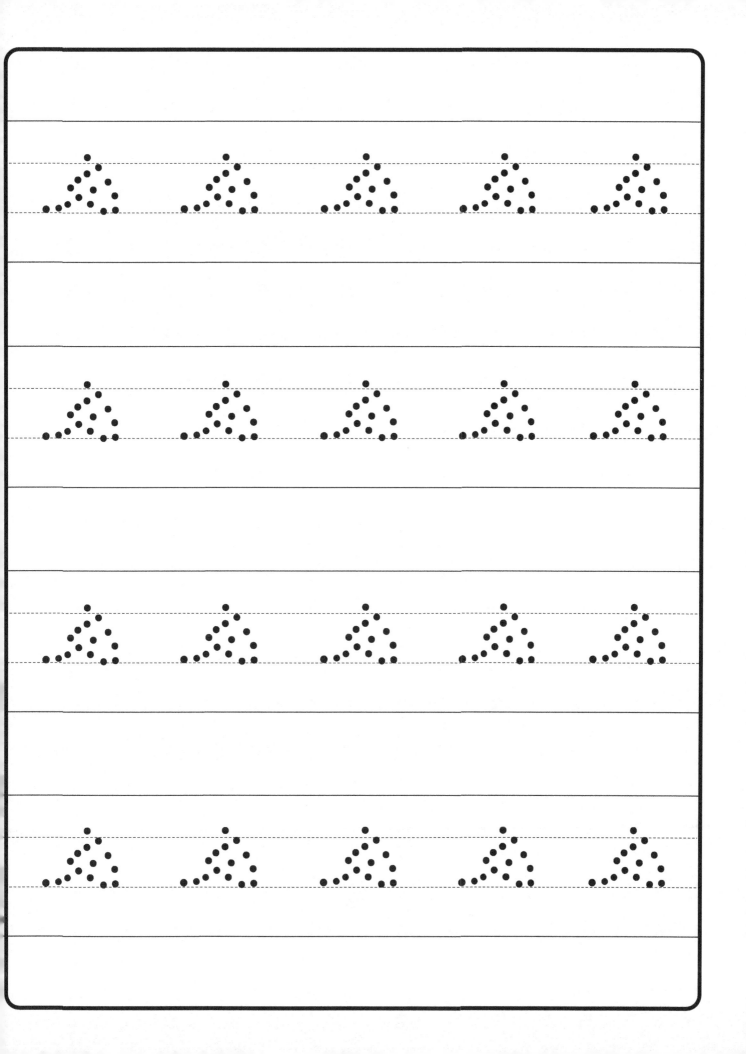

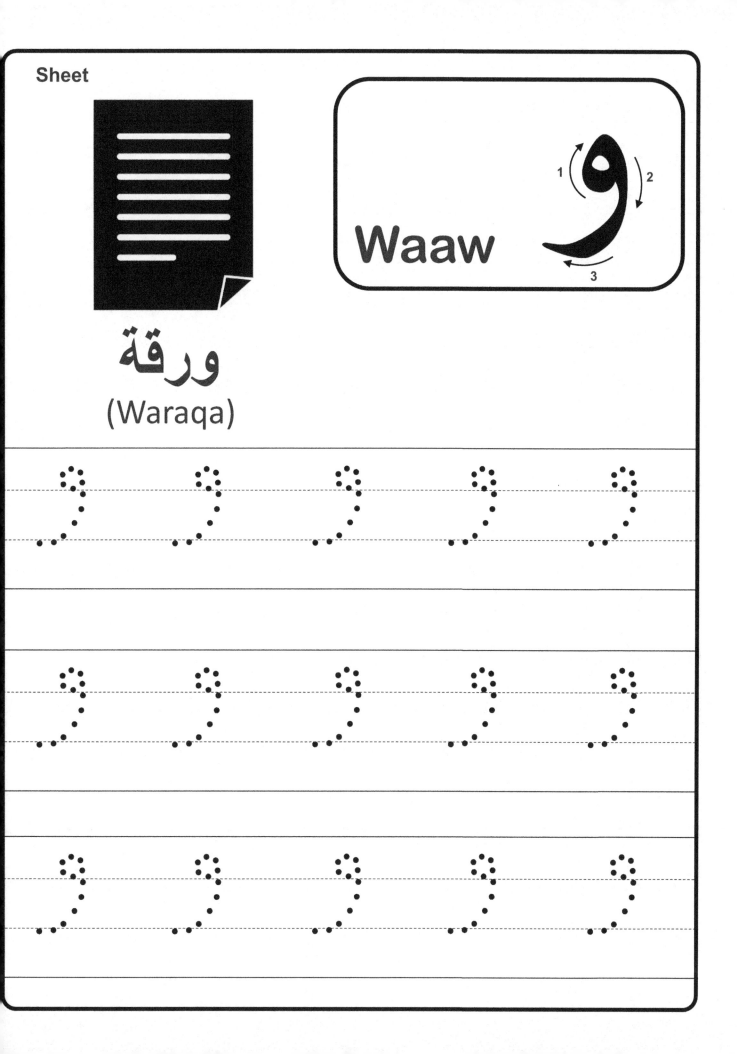

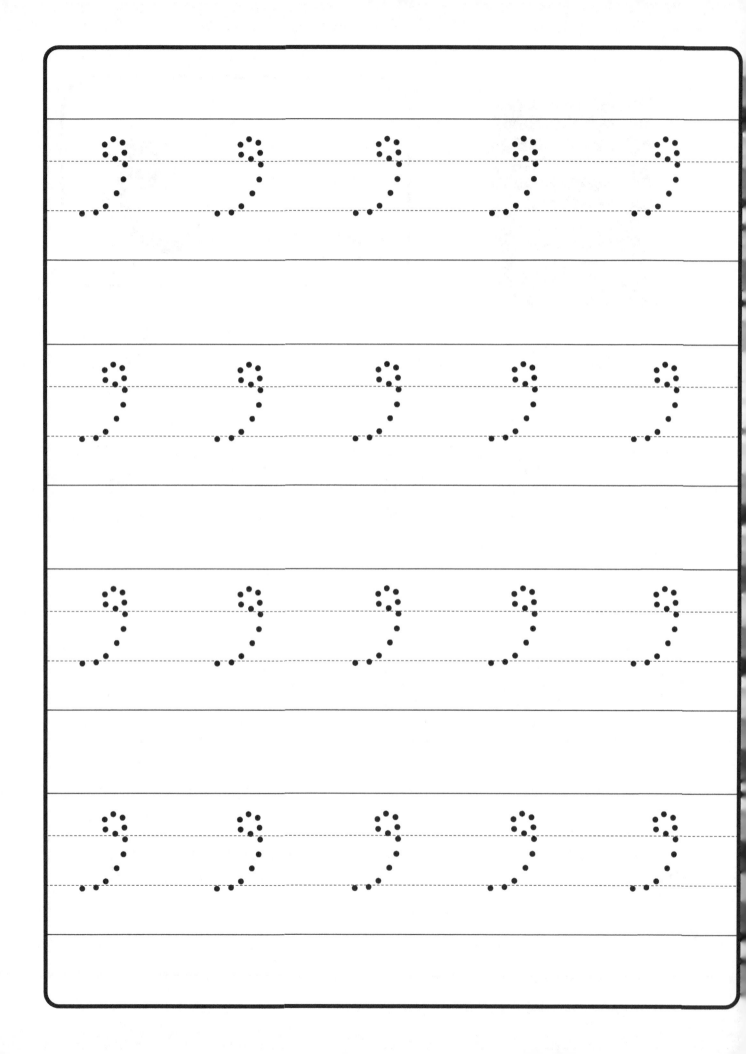

Hand

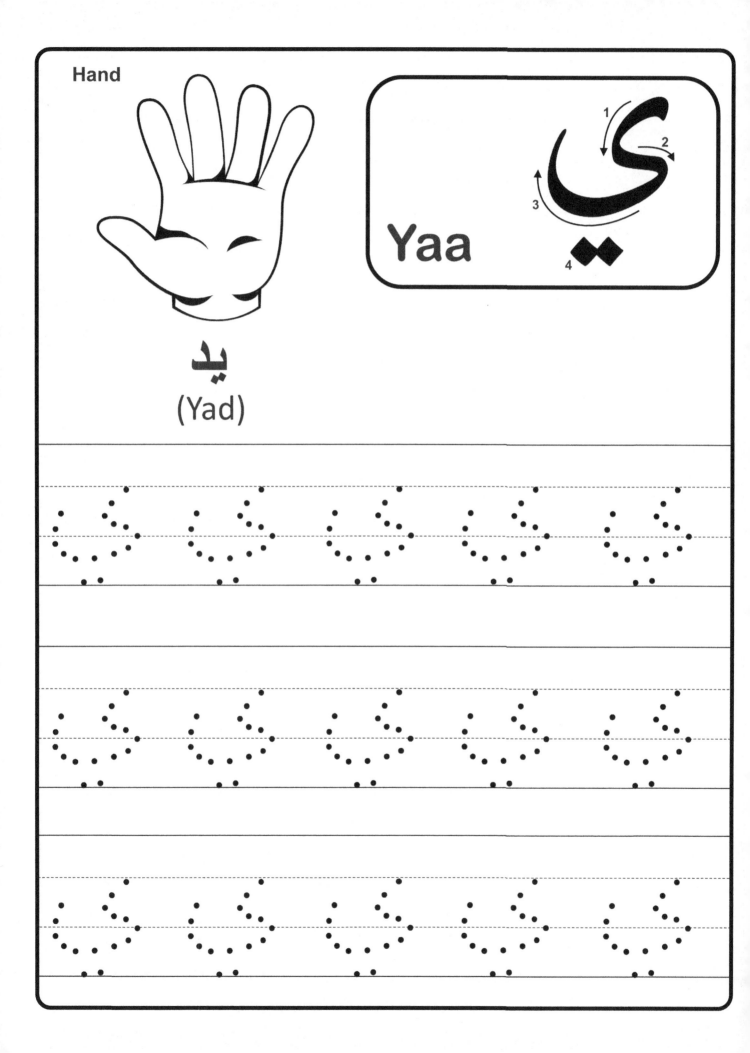

يد
(Yad)

Yaa

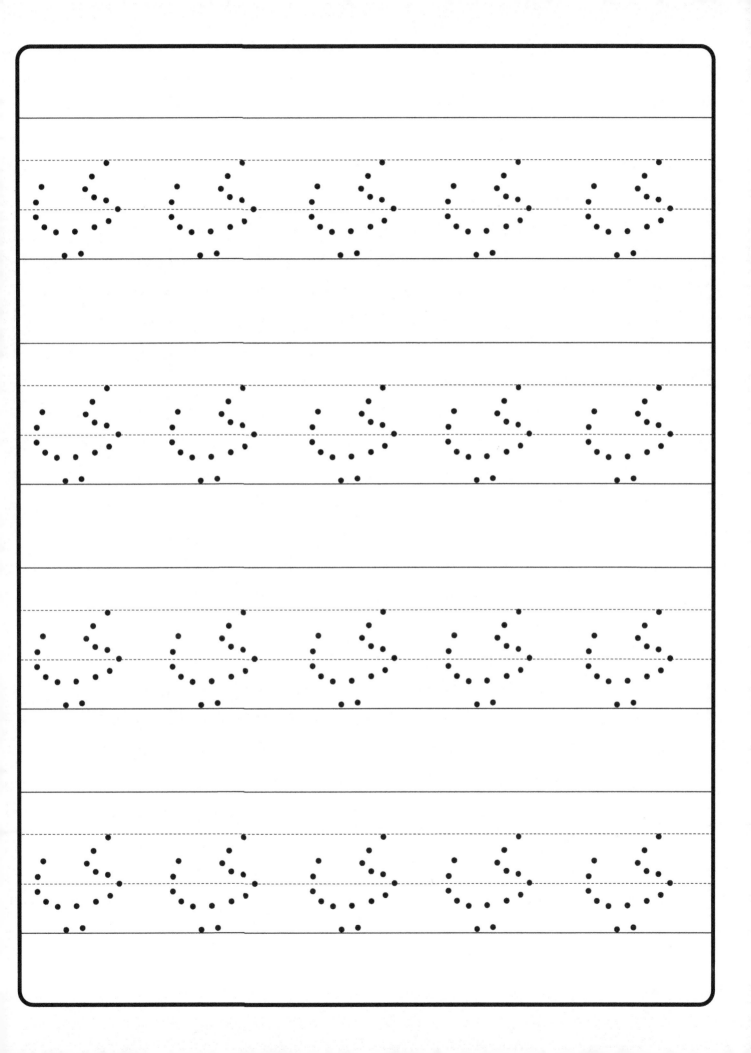

Part 03

Tracing The
Arabic Numbers

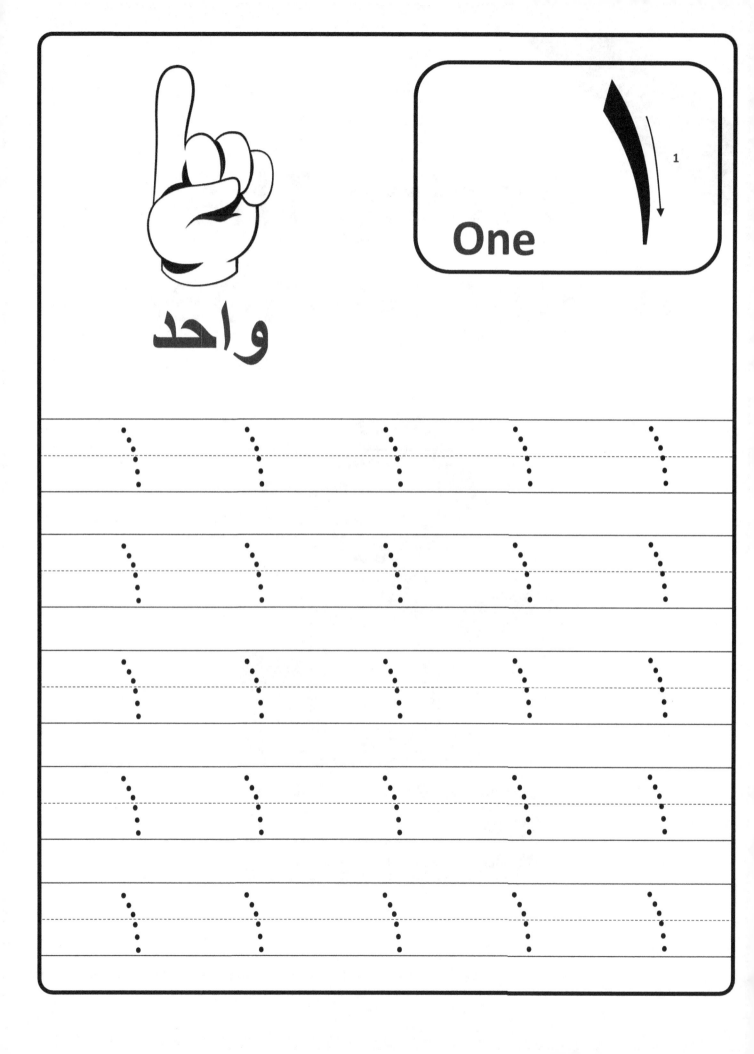

واحد

One

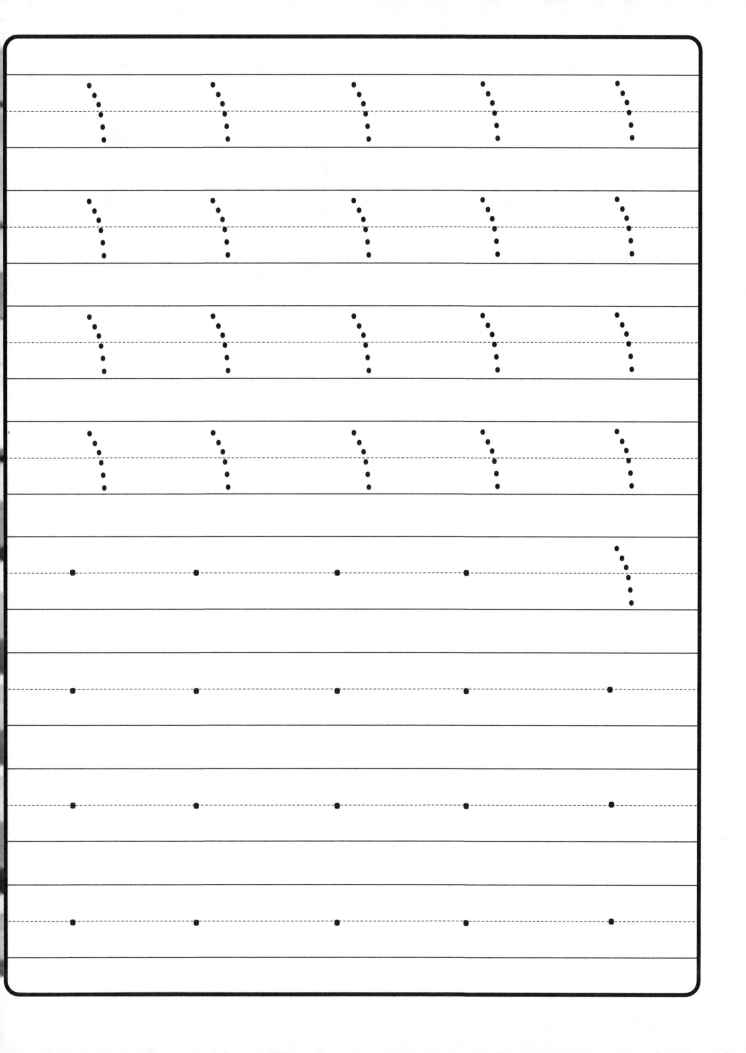

اثنان

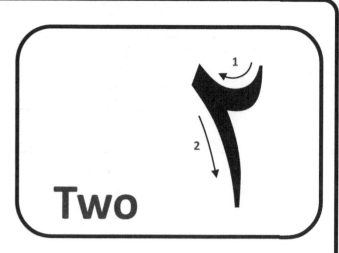

Two

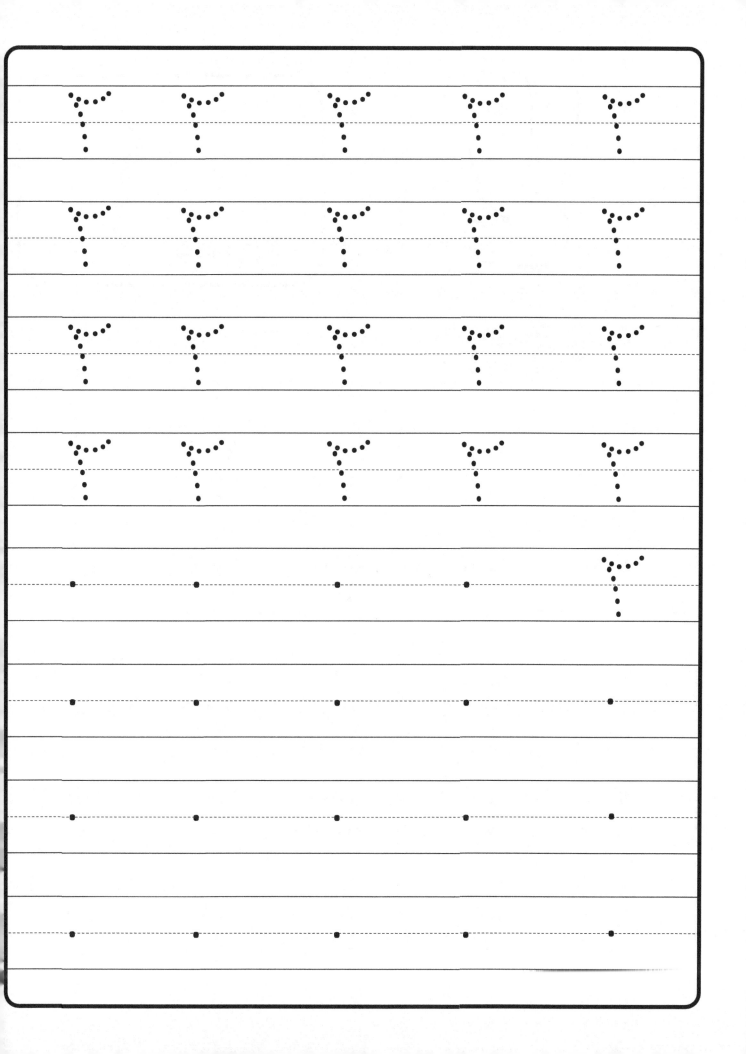

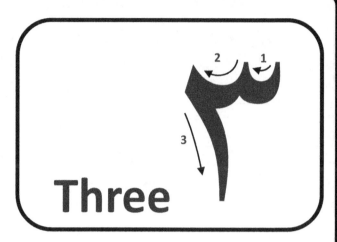

Three

ثلاثة

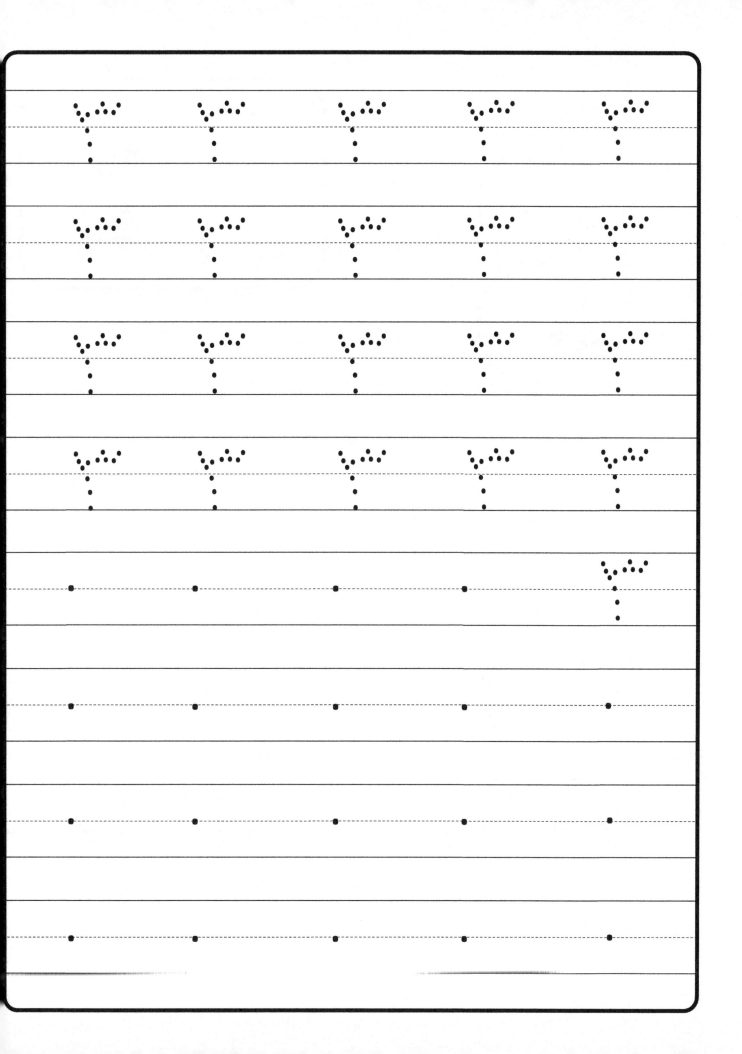

أربعة

Four

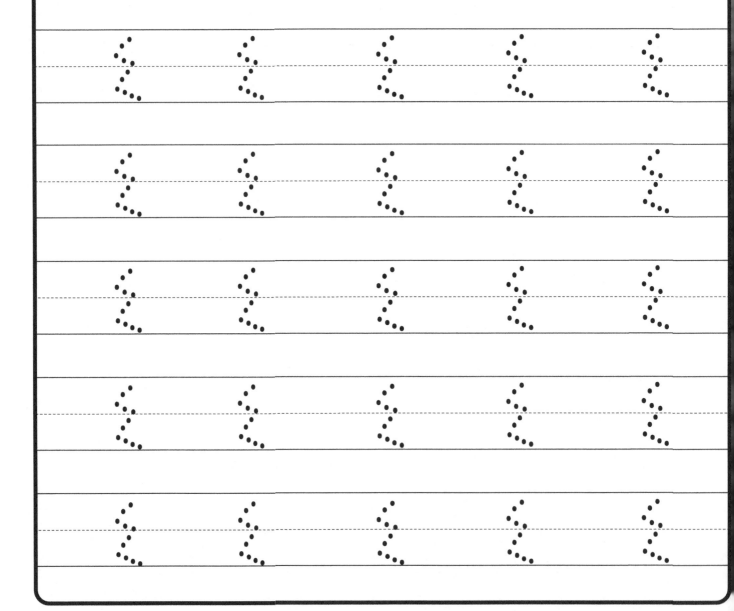

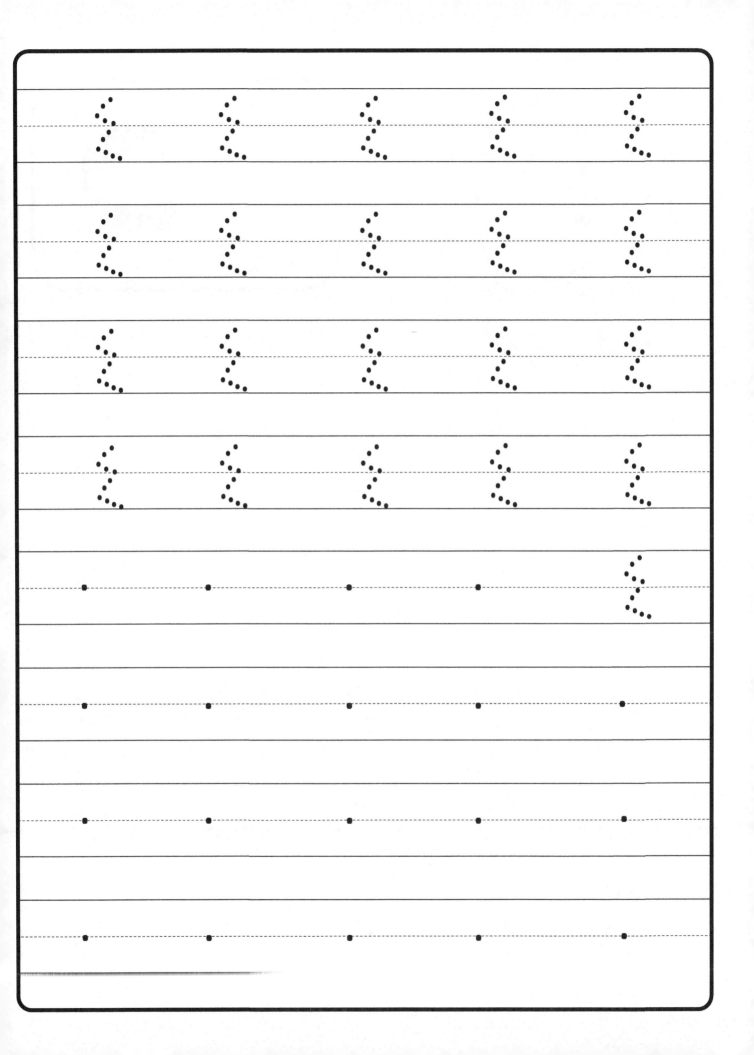

خمسة

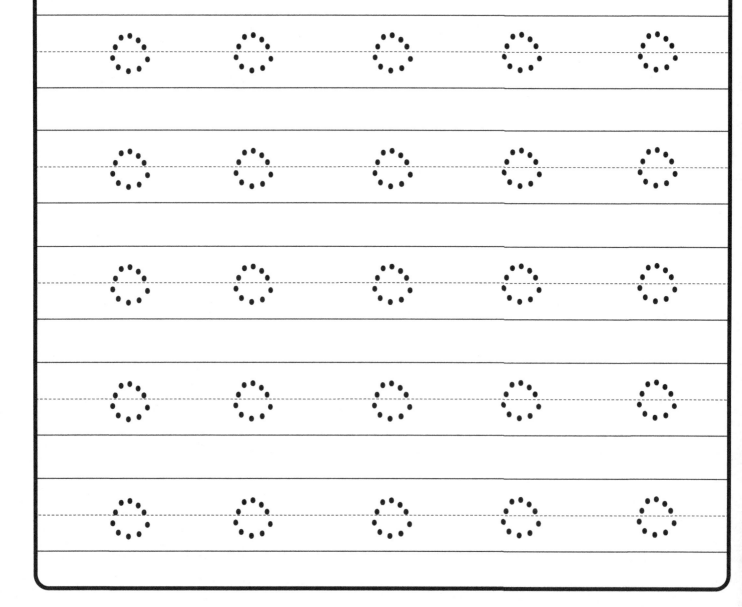

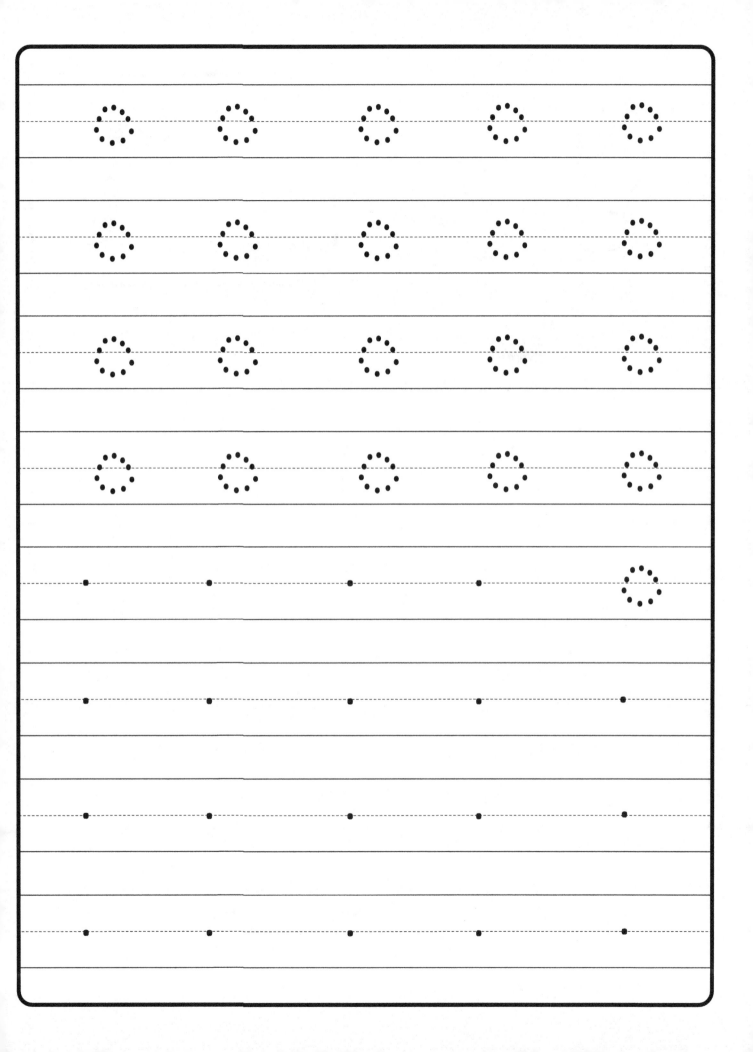

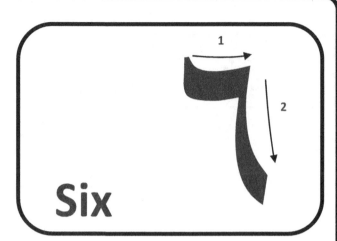

Five

Six

ستة

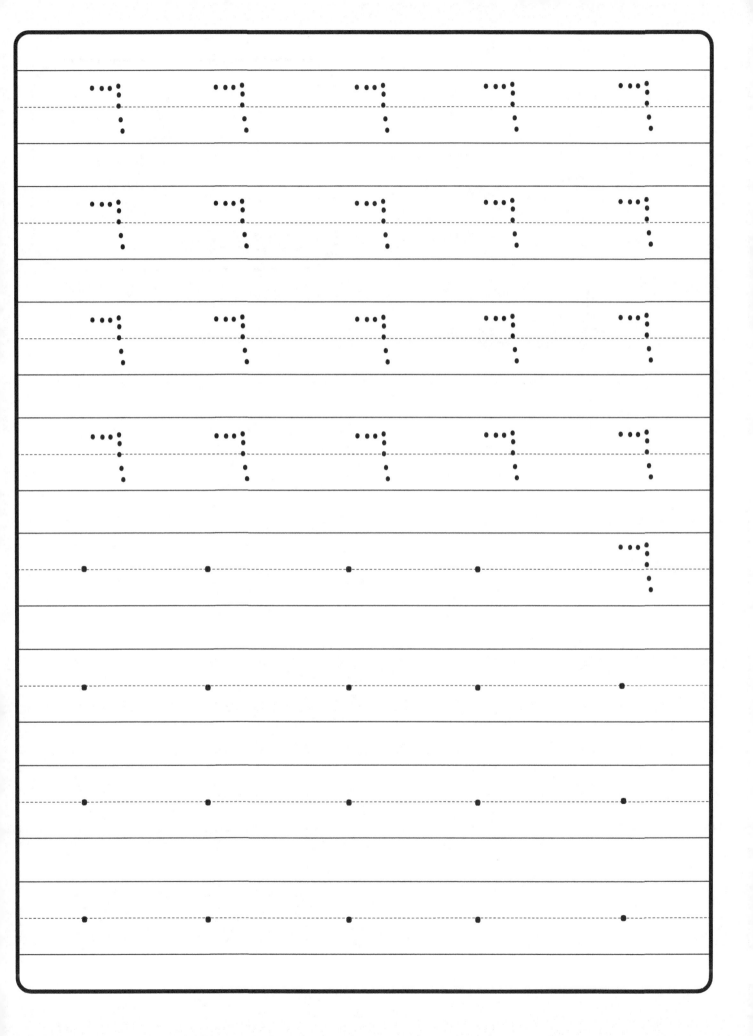

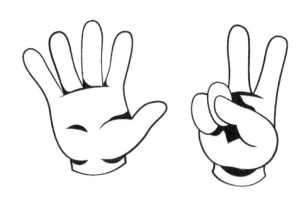

سبعة

Seven

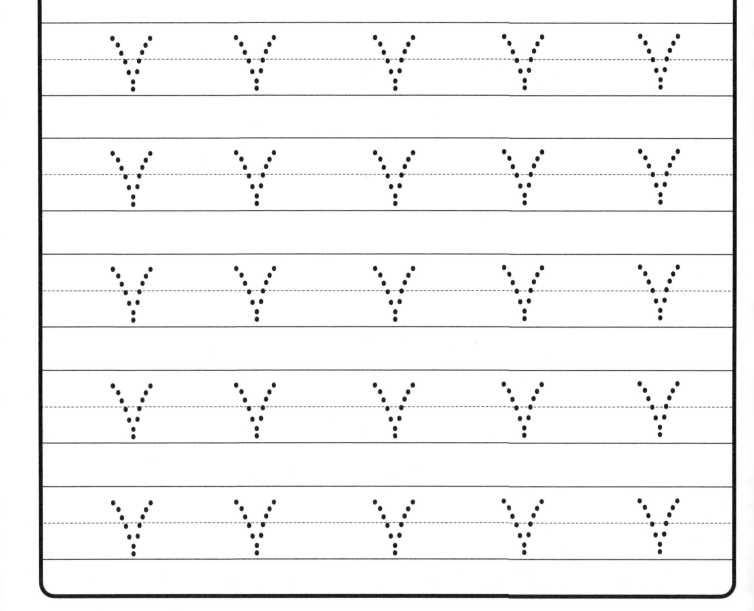

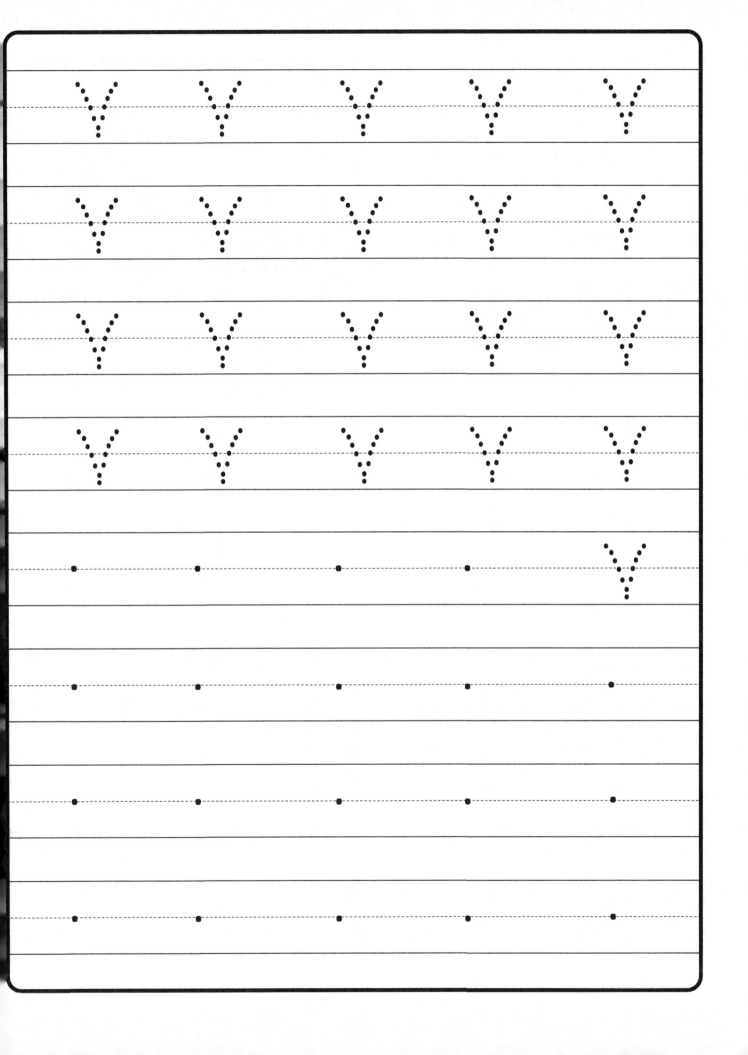

Eight

ثمانية

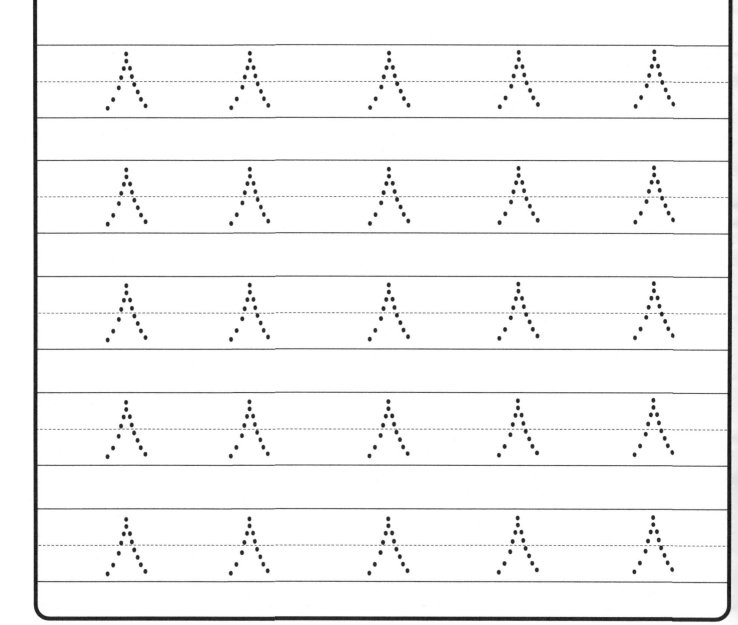

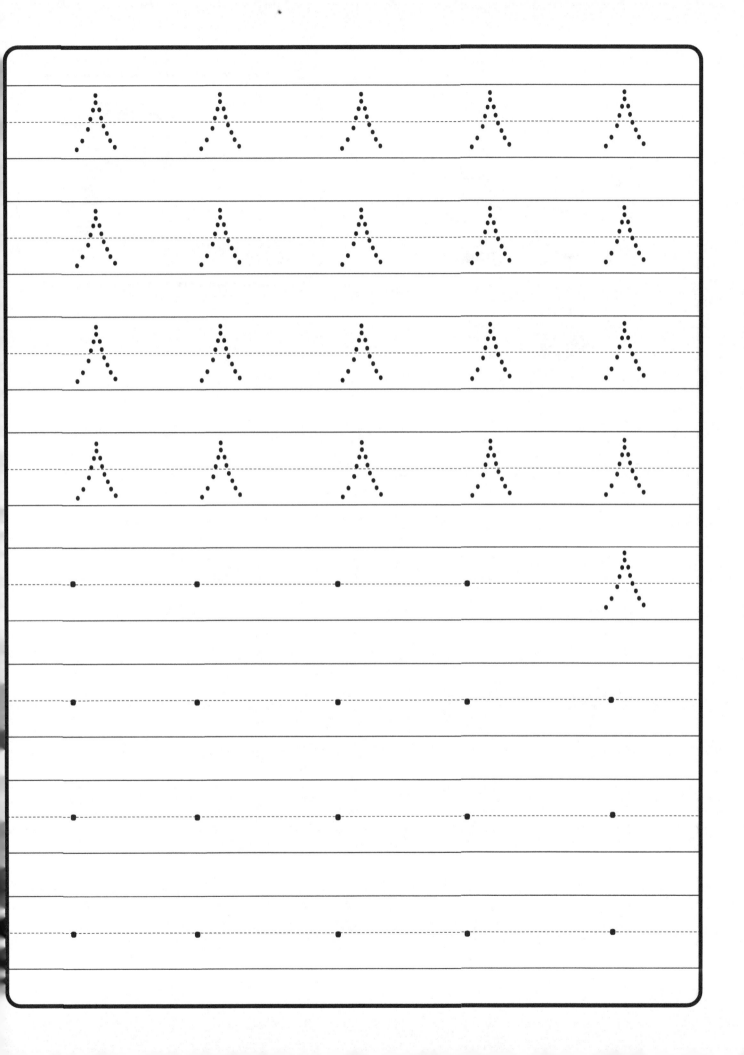

تسعة

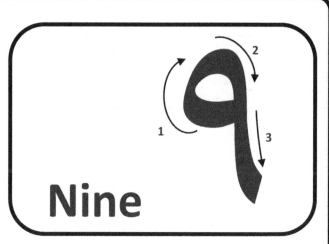

Nine

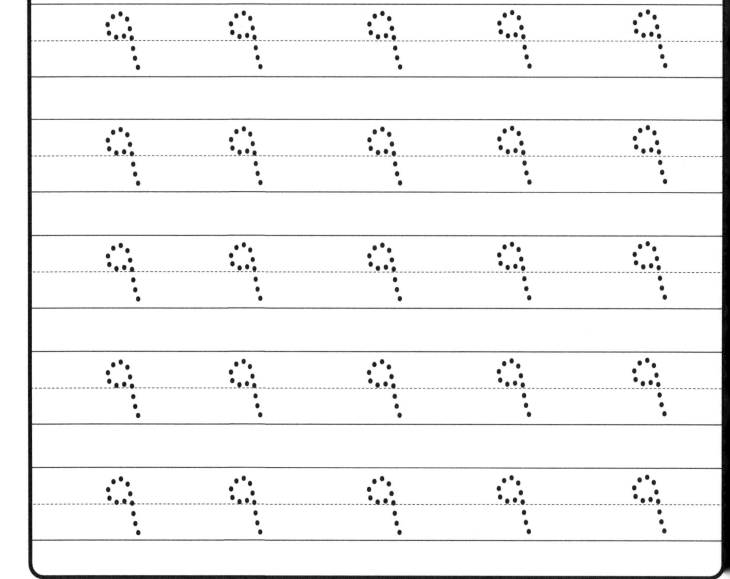

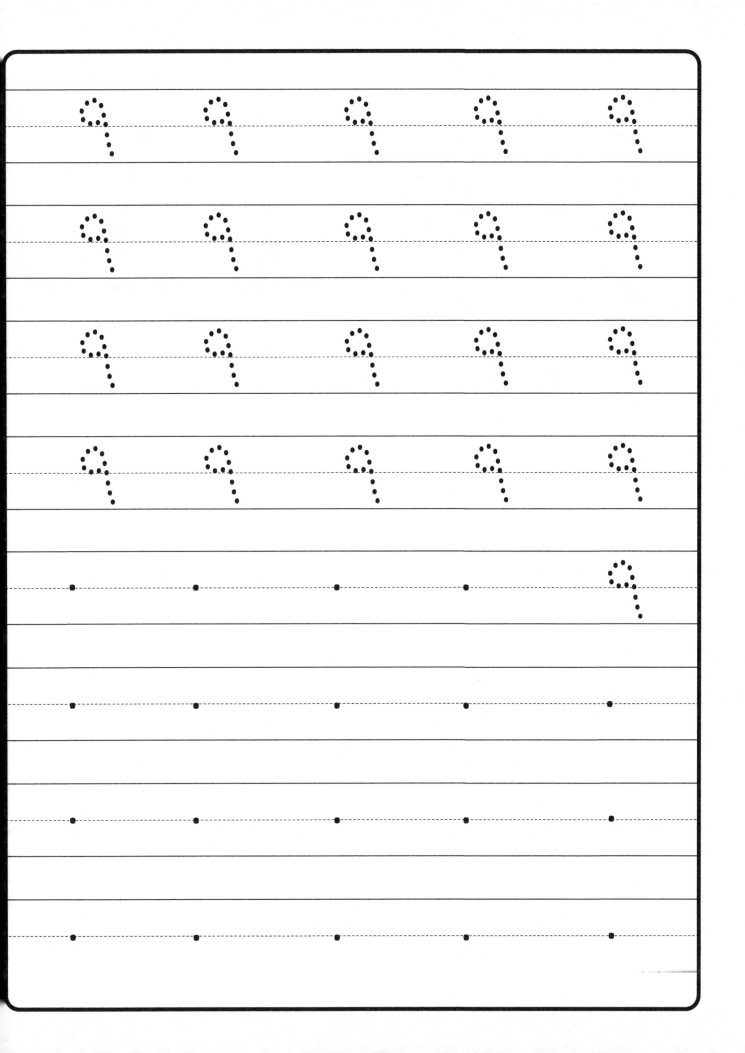

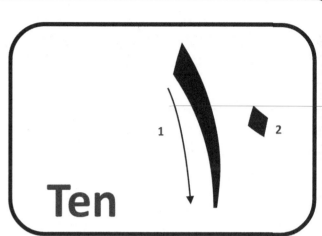

Ten

عشرة

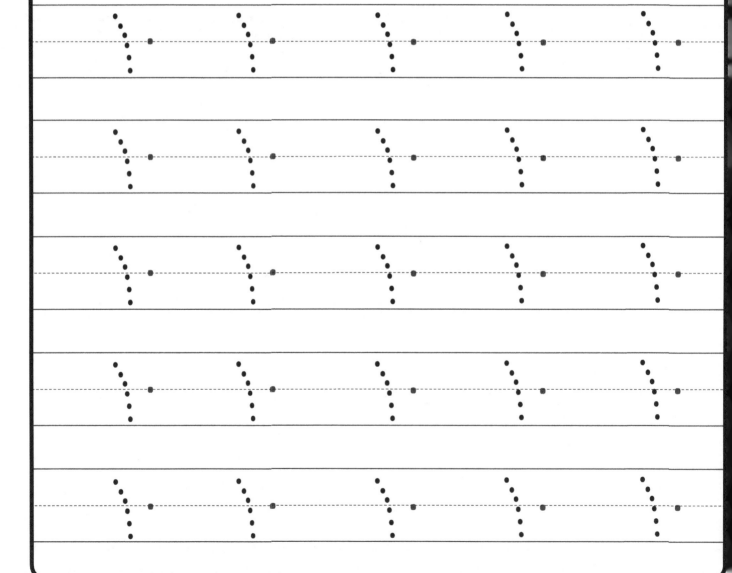

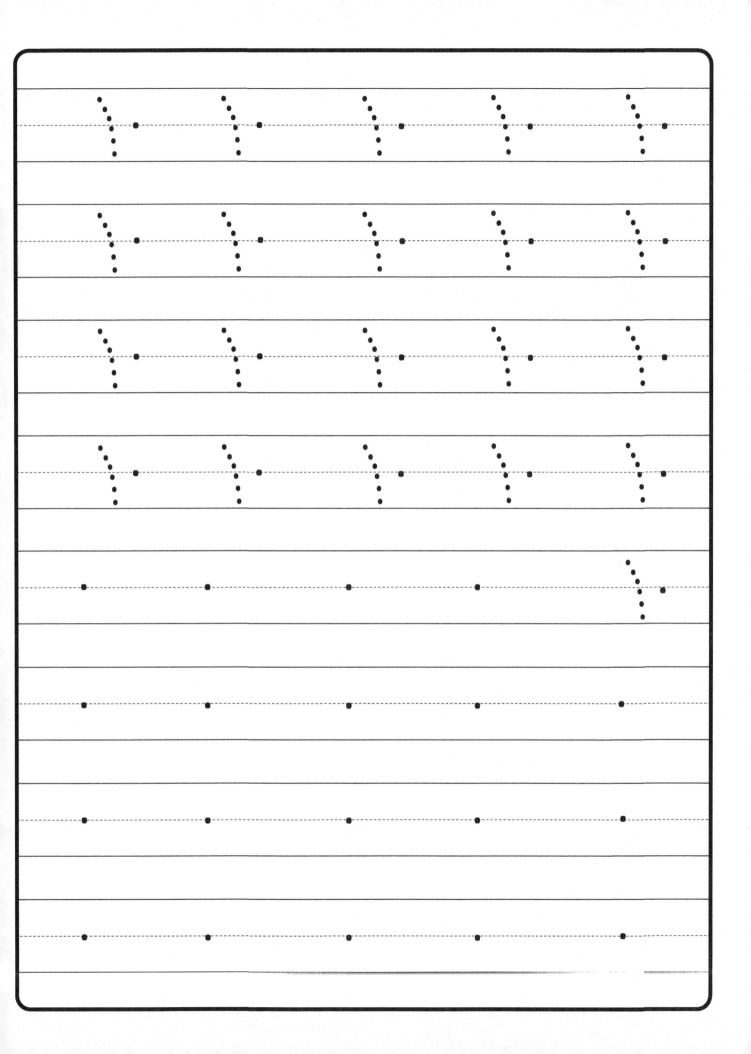

Certificate of
Achievement

Awarded to

....

Signed: ....

Date: ....

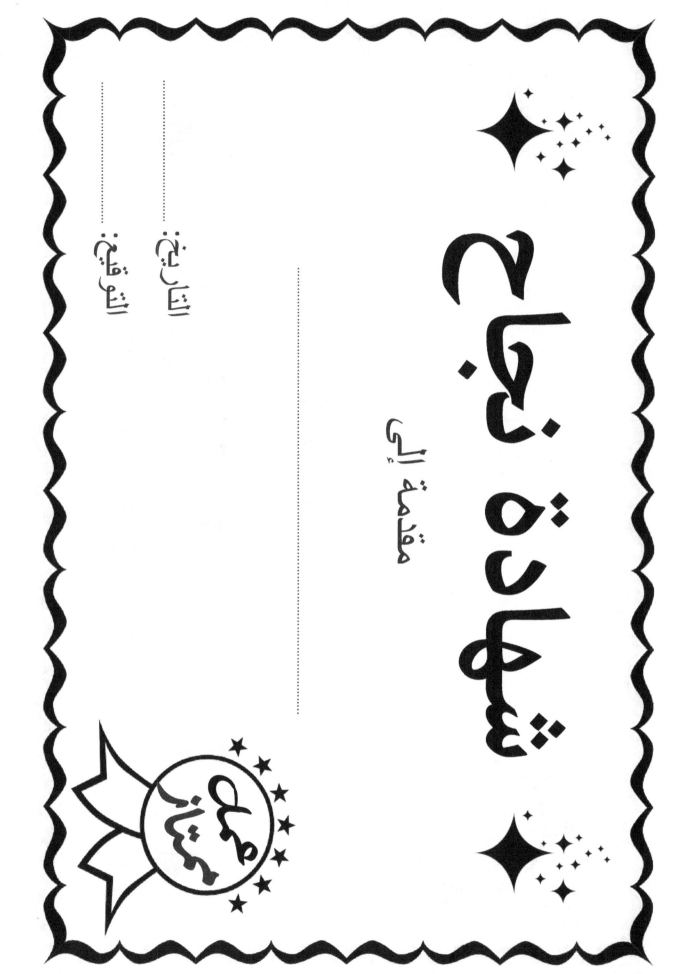

بطاقة تهنئة

مقدمة إلى ......

إلى : ....

من : ....

Important Information:

This workbook is a labor of love. Accordingly, if you're a student of Arab,

a teacher, or homeschooling your children, I grant you the non-commercial

right to photocopy any part of this workbook for your own or your students,

personal use.

Finally, we'd like to know what you think!

If you liked this book, please leave me a review on Amazon!
Your kind reviews and comments will encourage me to make more books
like this.

Thank you
Isaac Design

Questions & Customer Service:
Email us at isaacdesign4kids@gmail.com

Made in the USA
Columbia, SC
23 October 2024

44911919R00070